The author's proceeds from this book will help Catholic Mission's work, the Pontifical Mission Societies' giving of practical, spiritual and emotional support to communities of most need in more than one hundred and sixty countries.

First impression 500 copies 2001
Second impression February 2002

Cover: Father John Lisle (as a young curate) relaxes at Holy Trinity Stroud Green in London.

Published by *Access Press*
P.O. Box 446, Bassendean, Western Australia 6054

Copyright © *John Logan with Father John Lisle*, 2001

This book is copyright. Apart from any fair dealing for the purpose of private study, research, criticism or review, as permitted under the Copyright Act, no part may be reproduced by any process without written permission. Enquiries should be made to the publisher.

Typesetting, layout and design by *Access Press*

National Library of Australia
Cataloguing in Publication data
Tall Order
ISBN 0 86445 151 2

Distributed in Australia and Overseas by the Publisher.

TALL ORDER

A JOURNEY TO TRUTH

John Logan with Father John Lisle

IMPRIMATUR:
Most Rev B J Hickey
Perth, WA. June 2001

I, Father John Lisle,
dedicate this book to the memory of
my beloved wife Mary

Foreword

It is intriguing how two Anglican missionaries in the Bahamas have had a significant impact on the Catholic Church in Western Australia.

One was Monsignor John Hawes, known as the Hermit of Cat Island. Having spent some years in the Bahamas as an Anglican missionary, he became a Catholic, then a Catholic priest, and worked for many years in the Diocese of Geraldton before returning to the Bahamas where he spent his last years. His heritage in Western Australia is evident in the numerous churches he designed as an architect and, in some cases, built with his own hands.

The other is the subject of this book, Father John Lisle. To some extent a contemporary of John Hawes, though much younger, he too was an Anglican missionary in the Bahamas who settled eventually in the Archdiocese of Perth as a Catholic priest.

His life is truly fascinating. From his pioneering days among the people of the Bahamas he went to South Africa as a missionary and then to England for a short time. The next move was to the Anglican Diocese of Bunbury where he settled with his wife and family. It was there that he made his approach to the local Catholic Bishop to become a Catholic, and a married Catholic priest at that. History was made there with Rome accepting not one but three former Anglican priests for ordination as Catholic priests.

We read of the difficulties and the joys of such an unheard of transition as Father Lisle and his family began this new adventure into the community and the parish life of the Catholic Church.

What makes this book so readable is that each phase of Father Lisle's life is brought to life by a wealth of stories, stories that he enjoyed telling the author and that clearly still keep him amused and happily grateful to God for a life full of graces and blessings.

Most Rev B J Hickey
Archbishop of Perth

Acknowledgement

When I decided to help Father John Lisle to recount his life experiences in a book I had no idea that so many people from so many different walks of life would volunteer to be involved.

I thought my fellow Catholics would be interested in the project and that some of them would be in a position to offer their services, which turned out to be the case, but I doubted whether people outside the Church would be keen to lend a hand.

How far off track my line of thinking proved to be.

I was helped and encouraged by non-Christians as well as Christians from various faiths in a way which will long be remembered.

Whether people initially got involved because of the nature of the book or because they knew Father Lisle or me doesn't matter. It is far more important that they felt comfortable participating in a story about a man with an evident belief in God and an open, loving approach towards fellow human beings.

I thank you all from my heart for helping.

Tireless workers included Reformed Churches of Australia pastors Johann Joubert and Peter Abetz, researcher Morgan Jones, journalist David Cooper and all-rounder Richmond Derham.

Special thanks also to my family and Father Lisle's for their encouragement over the four years it took to produce Tall Order.

John W. Logan

John W. Logan

Preface

My indebtedness to John Logan who lovingly undertook to write my life story after spending many hours interrogating me. This story of my life is meant to be an inspiration for other people, and in no way a glorification of myself.

There are many people to be thanked but I know that John will faithfully remember them all. I only wish to make mention of one, and that is my beloved Archbishop who kindly wrote the foreword. In his foreword, he generously likens me to Fra Jerome better known to West Australians as Monsignor John Hawes. Fra Jerome was a wonderful priest and I am honoured to be compared to him.

I hope that this book of my experiences in life, particularly my conversion to the One True Faith, will be a source of inspiration to many, many people. I had no other intention of placing it down on paper than this.

God bless you all,

J E C Lisle

Father John E C Lisle

Contents

Foreword	v
Acknowledgement	vii
Preface	viii
Bahamas Adventure	1
South African Challenges	28
The Ugly Politics Behind Apartheid	38
Call to Become Catholics	51
First Married Catholic Priests	62
Early Parishes	74
Trials and Triumphs	85
The Death of my Beloved Mary	94
True Friends	103
Life from the Back Seat	112
Retirement and Reflections	118
The Way, Truth and Life	129
Bibliography	131

This is an
ACCESS PRESS
Publication

Bahamas Adventure

Andros

I looked at her as she approached, worried that I might fail to find the right words to console her. She was a mother about to lose a son at the hands of the hangman at Fox Hill Jail in Nassau, capital of the Bahamas.

I was the jail's chaplain and, as such, had become familiar with hangings. One of my regular routines was to counsel killers and then witness them gasp their last breath.

Joseph Flowers, aged 30 something, was to be hanged for a single murder but he had told me that he had killed at least a dozen people. I was sure Mrs Flowers had come to say her goodbyes and I could only hope and pray that my words would help her to come to terms with Joseph's fate.

She said: "I've come to collect Joseph's bicycle. After he's hanged I can sell it to make some money."

I guess I shouldn't have been surprised because that was the kind of crude attitude the Negroes had in the Bahamas. It was difficult to find out how much they loved one another, if at all.

The black Africans, or Negroes, were not indigenous to the Bahamas, but had been transported to the islands by the Spanish to be their slaves. The islands' original inhabitants had been murdered by Spaniards during their search for land and fortune to claim on behalf of their sovereign.

Even though the Negroes eventually got to be a free people, poverty was so extreme that life was cheap.

It was clear to me that people like Flowers were to some extent victims of the conditions in which they were raised.

I had arrived in the Bahamas from England on a ship about six years earlier. It was on the feast of the epiphany in 1949. My first assignment as a raw 30-year-old Anglo-Catholic priest was on the island of Andros, more of an archipelago, with just lay assistant Gordon Bennett, 28, to help me. He had been a friend for many years and was to be a tower of strength in the primitive surrounds. I was in charge of twelve separate parishes with twelve churches. There were no roads on Andros, just bush tracks, and no vehicles.

Gordon and I went about on a seven metre sailing boat, with the help of a captain and his mate, and rode a horse - the only one on the island. We relied on two small shops for supplies and learnt to eat easy-to-prepare basic foods. The rectory was like a wooden rabbit hutch. At least we had sanitary, unlike the locals, but I was nervous about sitting on the outside loo because of scorpions.

There were just two other white people on Andros - a Victoria Cross recipient from World War I, Group Captain Reece, who was in his 70s and had married a young Negress he had put in the family way, and Roman Catholic priest Father Alto.

Nothing in the eight years I had spent as curate at Holy Trinity Stroud Green in England could have prepared me for the God-forsaken world we were to call our home for more than two years. Gordon and I had many anxious moments during safaris from our base at the island's major centre, Mangrove Cay.

Andros had once been a glorious coral reef - it almost certainly had been formed by the sea subsiding leaving behind a terrain so rocky that it had to be seen to believed. Somehow each of the twelve settlements, each with their own church, had been developed on rock. It was painfully difficult for us to get around the parishes. We managed to get to them by boat, but we never knew what we would find when we arrived.

We were born and raised in England, one of the most civilised countries of the world, and had little idea about what the black

Father Lisle at Mangrove Cay on Andros riding the only horse on the island

Andros youngsters unload luggage for Father Lisle on his arrival at a settlement

Gordon Bennett chats with Andros children

people of Andros thought of us, especially in the initial stage of shifting and settling in our new home.

Thank God there were a few light-hearted times which eased the mental strain.

On one safari to Staniard Creek, one of the bigger settlements on Andros, we were greeted by the catechist holding a notebook on the parish's finances.

"These are the things that I've spent money on Father," he said. "A lot of money has gone on candles and a casket and supplies."

He had a serious face so I surmised he wasn't joking.

"Casket and supplies, what do you mean?" I asked.

"You know Father, the long black thing you wear in church and the other thing you wear over it," he replied.

Gordon and I found it impossible to hold back tears as we laughed and laughed. The catechist was referring to a priest's cassock and surplice.

Unperturbed by our reaction, the catechist handed me a long list of names and addresses. "These are the names of all the local bad people - the people you shouldn't visit," he told me.

I took the list from him saying: "Thanks, these will be the starting names of the many people that I'll call on."

He was dumbfounded. He might have had good intentions but obviously knew little about pastoral care. On the other hand, the list could have been the names of people with whom he had fallen out - I thought this was much more likely to be the case.

I was more troubled by another catechist, from a settlement called Pure Gold, than by him. I did not have a clue where the name came from because there was none of the precious metal to be found on Andros or anything which even resembled it. Pure Gold's catechist was a drunkard and I wanted the Anglican Church's hierarchy to remove him from the key parish post. I had no luck, my superiors deciding it was a matter for me to handle alone.

It was obvious to Gordon and I that he was far from the best person to manage the parish's finances and that he would have to go, but I procrastinated over sacking him. One day before I sacked him I was visiting a neighbouring settlement when I came across a couple of friendly faces. One of them was the local schoolteacher and the other was his wife. "Father, how are you getting on at Pure Gold?" the woman asked. "I tell you in all honesty, I'm glad to get away from that place," I said. "I've had enough of that drunken old catechist." She smiled. "Yes, I know he's a problem. He's my father."

A lot of work was needed to improve the spiritual lives of Andros people. I couldn't help but notice that some local beliefs were primitive, to say the least. There was a lot of voodooism, called obeah, practiced by the islanders. They were petrified of evil spirits and believed certain rituals, which included hanging bottles in certain trees, would help to protect them.

A strapping policeman came to visit one day and stayed too long, for him anyway. It was dark by the time he was ready to set off for home and fear got the better of him. He asked Gordon to accompany him past a spirit tree. It was a good thing Gordon obliged or he would never have gone home.

Gordon and I looked forward to seeing *The Gary Roberts*, a passenger boat which also brought everything from mail and supplies to furniture to Andros. The vessel was our one regular means of communicating with family, friends and the Church's chiefs. Our only other way of staying in touch with the modern world was via an amphibious plane which brought the occasional visitor to the island. Of course, very few locals had seen inside the plane. Andros people did not have enough money to be paying passengers on the boat or plane and even if they had a way to leave Andros, they wouldn't have wanted to venture outside their familiar surrounds.

I arranged the first visit ever of nuns to Andros because I thought it would be beneficial for the Negroes to meet them. The visit was designed to broaden the locals' appreciation of the Christian faith. But it got off to a wet start when one of the two Anglican ladies fell from the Mangrove Cay jetty.

Gordon and I had moved from the rectory to another house so the English nuns, based in Nassau, could use our facilities. We did not expect the mail boat to arrive at night but it did on the occasion that the two ladies were aboard. *The Gary Roberts* anchored some distance from shore and her passengers climbed down a ladder into dinghies - no mean feat for nuns in their habits.

I waited for our guests on the quay, which was in so much darkness it was difficult to see any more than about a metre. One of the nuns, Sister Bride, climbed out of her dinghy and started to run towards me. She didn't get far because, unbeknown to her, the jetty was not much wider than that of a standard footpath and it was easy to get too close to its edge. Down she went - splashhhhh! She obviously wasn't The Flying Nun.

As other members of the welcoming party hastened to fish her out of the briny, Sister Bride's companion joined me in fits of laughter. After they hauled Sister onto the jetty, she too burst into laughter - she obviously had a wonderful sense of humour. But the islanders were far from amused by the mishap. They had been looking forward to the visit for months and wanted a smooth, ceremonial arrival. Most of them looked to be shocked by the accident and I think many felt ashamed that a nun in her mid 40s had fallen from their jetty.

My Mangrove Cay parishioners put my faith in the Lord to the test a number of times.

I upset almost everyone in the community once by getting rid of the settlement's head teacher after I caught him intoxicated at the school several times. He also was giving alcohol to students. The Education Department at Nassau acted on my complaint by dismissing him. When the locals heard what I had done, many of them threatened to decapitate me with machetes - they liked him so much. The local parishioners boycotted attending the church for seventeen Sundays, leaving Gordon and me to celebrate Mass without them.

No one from the congregation told me why almost all of them returned to church on the 18th Sunday.

I think it was because their standards were so low that they couldn't see anything wrong with the teacher. Maybe they came round to my way of thinking because of the way we served them spiritually and physically, but it was impossible to learn what they believed.

It was becoming crystal clear to me why the American priest who had preceded me had fled back to civilisation after six months in the job.

The Andros locals, about 1000 people, had limited knowledge of the Western world. Most of them were far from being familiar with basic English. I'll never forget a baptism in Nichols Town, another of my parishes, when I asked the mother to inform me and the congregation of her baby's name. "Gonorrhoea, Father, that's it," she said without the blink of an eye. I nearly fell through the church's floor. "You can't call your child Gonorrhoea," I told her. "Why not?" she retorted. "Do you know what Gonorrhoea is?" I inquired. "Yes," she said. "It's a very pretty name."

Again I asked whether she was aware of what the word meant. Of course she didn't, so I tried to explain. "It's a disease which men catch from dirty women," I said. "You mean gentlemen's disease," she said.

Her fellow parishioners appeared dumbfounded by the carry on. I'm certain they were also unfamiliar with the word. Despite the formal occasion, I'm sure any Westerner would have found it impossible to hold back laughter. Fortunately, the mother settled on a more suitable name. I forget it, but would never forget the name she initially intended for her child.

I think in many ways Gordon found it more difficult than I to come to terms with the local way of life, despite his British army background in World War II. He worked tirelessly doing almost all of the medical work on Andros using skills he had acquired from the army's medical corps. But his frustration was evident. One time he carefully bandaged an arm of an injured man only to learn later that the patient unwrapped the bandages and replaced them with leaves.

The island was without a hospital and there were few medical facilities so locals turned to Gordon, especially when there was an emergency. Brother Gordon, as they called him, was not a doctor nor a miracle worker but sometimes he was left with impossible cases. Few, if any, of the sick or injured were flown to Nassau for medical treatment. If Gordon could not help them, they had to fend for themselves.

Late one summer's night, someone started banging on the front door of the rectory so Gordon and I went to see what was going on. We found a badly injured man lying on the steps to the house - whoever brought him to us had left. He had big thumb marks on his neck which appeared to have been the result of someone trying to strangle him. Gordon did as much as he could for him during the night. It was daytime before a doctor from Nassau arrived by plane - white people seldom rushed to the aid of a black person.

The doctor saw the man on the pier, where we had taken him so that he would be close to the plane when it landed, but walked past to our home. Putting the man on the jetty so he might get treated quickly had been a waste of time.

Gordon and I weren't impressed but we thought it wise to be polite. I offered the doctor a cup of tea, hoping he would say no and get on with treating the man or at worst have a quick cuppa. He thanked me and then proceeded to take his time drinking tea and scoffing cake while the man was left in the heat unattended. Gordon and I were never to know what became of our injured visitor. After the doctor eventually left Andros with him, he could have died. No one seemed to care.

House at Mangrove Cay

I had learnt some useful medical practices soon after we arrived on Andros. One experience at Mangrove Cay remained clear in my memory for a long time. I had encountered a big Negro who wanted a tooth extracted from the back of his mouth. "I can't possibly do that," I said.

"You won't be any use unless you can," he snarled.

I then decided to travel to Nassau for elementary lessons in dentistry.

Most people worked as fishermen and sponge gatherers or grew yams between coral rocks by putting soil into clefts. The islanders' poverty was apparent by the clothes they wore - such as flour sacks which had been made into shirts. They lived in shacks built from wood and compressed earth, and eventually their nearby excrement was washed away by torrential rains and eaten by scavenger birds. Brothers and sisters cohabited in overcrowded huts. The amount of incest was frightful.

We shared the value of the boat with the people in as much as our vessel, the *St Clement*, was vital to do our work. We relied on the *St Clement* to at times negotiate mountainous seas. The former fishing boat graced the archipelago with the papal flag flying from her mast. I suppose we were more Catholic than Anglican. I also had a photograph of the Holy Father at the back of a church, which Bishop of Nassau Spence Burton got wind of. Bishop Burton, a short and well-built American, sent for me.

"Father, I understand you've got a picture of the Pope at the back of a church and you've got written underneath it, 'the chief pastor'," he said. "I want you to take it down because, as an Anglican, you know what the Pope thinks of you." He handed me a big photograph of himself to replace the one of the Pope.

"This is a much bigger picture of a much smaller man," I said. Outspoken remarks like that often got me into trouble.

I blessed the fishing boats annually and I thought it would be a good idea to build a shrine of Our Lady and face it towards the sea. On the day the Pope defined the Assumption as an article of faith, I led a big service on the island. I had started the Children of Mary, a group of youngsters who wanted to learn about the Holy Mother. The group and four men, who carried the statue, led a procession of parishioners to the site where the shrine was set up.

Life was never dull on Andros but I relished whatever opportunities I got to go to Nassau because it was a chance to be in civilisation. During one visit, I met Monsignor John Hawes, an Anglican priest-turned-Catholic Franciscan.

Fra Jerome, as he was known in the Bahamas, was a remarkable man.

The British-born missionary and architect had literally built a huge reputation, especially in the Bahamas and in Western Australia. His work in WA included building the Catholic cathedral in Geraldton, the Northampton and Mullewa Catholic churches and several convents and schools. Earlier, he had built a number of churches in the Bahamas as an Anglican priest, including St Paul's, which withstood a big hurricane. He returned to the Bahamas in the 1930s and built a Franciscan hermitage on Cat Island. His other works as a Catholic priest in the Bahamas included the Nassau cathedral and monastery. I met Fra Jerome at the monastery when I

Anglican Bishop of Nassau Spence Burton

Father Lisle aboard the St Clement with the captain, his mate and a houseboy

called on the monks. I enjoyed visiting them - it made no difference that I was Anglican and they Catholic.

"Would you like to meet Fra Jerome?" one of them asked me.

"Could I? Indeed, I would very much," I replied.

He directed me to where I found Fra Jerome lying on a bench wearing a pair of dirty jeans and a tattered shirt. I thought it was rather odd to see him dressed in such a way because I knew he was a cultured man. He was elderly but in reasonable health. I felt comfortable being with him - he was a very welcoming gentleman. Our paths were to cross several times over the next few years before he died in the United States in 1956.

God alone knows what or how much we achieved in our two years on Andros. I guess there must have been some pluses because the locals had come to trust us. They gathered at the quay and sang God Be With You Till We Meet Again when we left. I was bound to be parish priest of St Anne's in Nassau.

Gordon was to take a different Christian journey. He had been accepted by Bishop Burton to study to be a priest at a theological college in Barbados. The Church had decided his love and commitment on the primitive island earned him a chance to fulfil a lifelong ambition.

Nassau

I had never dreamt that petrol fumes could smell so good. Soaking up the modern world again was an experience which was to stay indelibly in my memory for many years.

Nassau had five parish churches and Christ Church Cathedral, where Bishop Burton was based. My manifold duties included a job as part-time chaplain at Fox Hill Jail as well as full-time parish priest of St Anne's.

One of the first obstacles that I encountered in the city was that the car of St Anne's former priest had been left to his mother in Wales. I informed my parishioners of the problem from the pulpit one Sunday and implored them to pray, saying if they did so the Lord would provide a vehicle for the parish. Next Saturday I returned home after shopping to find a woman standing in the churchyard adjoining the rectory. She asked if I was Father John. When I replied in the affirmative, she inquired: "Is there anything I can do for you?"

"Yes, there is. You can buy me a car," I said.

"I bloody well will," she told me.

The rough diamond was a British millionaire, Marion Carstairs. She ordered a Ford Prefect and ensured it was delivered to me so it could be blessed at the annual blessing of local vehicles the following Sunday.

Marion also opened an Anglican seminary door for John Taylor, who had been a close friend since I arrived in the Bahamas with Gordon. A generous endowment from Marion saw John, a former newspaper reporter married to another local, Coral, fulfil his lifelong wish to be an Anglican priest.

Gordon visited me in Nassau after passing exams in Barbados to be a deacon. He was well on his way to fulfilling his goal to become a priest and I was delighted for him. He had worked tirelessly with me on Andros and our many and varied experiences were anything but forgotten.

He was bound for Antigua to be ordained a priest, but his only immediate means of travel was aboard a Greek cargo ship. When I went to Nassau port to farewell my friend, I was invited to inspect his cabin. I found a chamber pot in its cabinet and could not resist putting it on my head to imitate a blessing by Greek orthodox archbishops. The fun ended in embarrassment when the captain knocked on the door and walked inside the cabin.

Nassau had its fair share of wealthy part-time residents. One of them with whom I formed a friendship was Scottish whisky baron Sir Jack McTaggart. He owned a house, to be more accurate a mansion, near my parish. Despite Sir Jack's mountain of money,

I found him to be a middle-aged man with a special rustic charm and I often enjoyed a meal in his home. His wife, Betty, died in Scotland and her body was cremated, but Sir Jack wanted her ashes laid to rest in a grave adjacent to St Anne's.

After a church service led by Bishop Burton, we carried the urn to the gravesite. We were short on cremation experience and were uncertain about how we should place the urn in the grave. I jumped in and was handed it while the Bishop continued to pray. A woman who delighted in knowing everyone's business, and who lived opposite the cemetery, did not see me descend into the grave. The Bishop and mourners forgot that I was "six foot under" and left me to find my own way out. I was not tall enough to climb out of the grave so I decided to make the most of the vessel containing the dearly departed's ashes, standing on it as I scratched my way to the surface in my white surplice. Apparently the busybody almost died of fright at the ghostly apparition which rose from the grave.

It wouldn't surprise me if Mrs McTaggart smiled down on the scene from her lofty point in the heavens.

I also wondered if my unexpected appearance made a difference to the church's collection plate, which I got altar servers to pass around the busybody's house as part of their duties because she used to watch the service with friends from her porch instead of joining other people in the community building.

Captain Reece, of Andros, died while I was St Anne's parish priest and was given a State funeral. How to treat his unrefined widow was a problem. No one wished ill of her but one could not help smiling at the experience she had sitting on a chair under trees near Christ Church Cathedral. When the defence forces fired three times in a 21-gun salute she was covered with leaves and dirty twigs until she resembled a compost heap rather than a dignified widow.

Work at the prison - separate male and female complexes with a raft of inmates from first offenders to serial killers - became

Fox Hill Jail's chapel

more of a full-time role and St Anne's part-time.

Two years after I arrived at Nassau, Bishop Burton decided that I was to concentrate all my efforts on Fox Hill's population, appointing me as the jail's first full-time chaplain. I was to hold the job for eight years, until 1959. I ran classes in reading, writing and arithmetic as part of a challenging rehabilitation program. There were about 500 prisoners in the jail - almost all of them Negroes. Although the prison was overcrowded, many of the inmates were less than keen to finish their jail terms because they were well fed and watered - something they could not take for granted on the other side of the bars.

But murder meant the death penalty and at exactly 8am twenty-one days after conviction the guilty person was hanged. My friends outside the jail said they saw me as a bright-eyed, quick-moving Englishman in his mid 30s. I think it would have been impossible for them to have comprehended how difficult it could be to find the words to counsel a condemned man. Joseph

Flowers and a countless number of other killers were invariable friendly towards me. But waiting in a condemned inmate's cell for him to return from court seemed to last an eternity.

Flowers threw his arms around me and cried out: "Don't let them hang me Father."

I prayed for him and visited him every day for the three weeks before he was hanged. On the morning he was to pay the ultimate price for crime, I offered to hear his Confession and give him Holy Communion, as was par for the course for someone on their way to the gallows. Flowers wrote his name and date of birth and death in a Gideon Bible and handed it to me. A bag was placed over the head of the killer before he left his cell to meet the hangman. Flowers stopped momentarily during his final journey and asked a prison official to remove the bag.

"Can you please take the bag off my head so that I can look at Father's face once more. He was the only friend I ever had."

His request was denied.

Executions were done under the authority of the province marshal. He was accompanied by a doctor, (one of whom fainted), the prison superintendent and the turnkey. We assembled in the gallows room for a rehearsal on the eve of every execution. On the night before Flowers was hanged we broke the usual practice of using a sandbag, opting to tie the rope around the head of a willing warder. The dummy run almost ended in a disaster when the executioner, who was out of sight behind a curtain, somehow came within seconds of hanging the man. "Stop, you've got a live person," I yelled frantically.

When the warder learnt about his close call, he went pale - he went as white as snow. The hangman was also shocked out of his wits.

The mid 1950s marked the start of some of the happiest times in my private life. It was then that I met and married one of God's most beautiful human angels. Well, I'm bending the truth because our paths had crossed when Gordon and I were living on Andros, but the scene had not been conducive to romance. Mary Hughes, a former Liverpool lass seven years younger than I, was the assistant matron at a Nassau hospital who cared for me while I suffered from a bladder problem. My bladder dried up because I took too much of a drug for a boil on one of my buttocks. I was flown to hospital and, after receiving treatment, my waterworks returned with a vengeance, leaving my bed and me soaked.

Our romance was kick-started by a Salvation Army captain who I thought I was in love with. She said we could never marry because of our different faiths but that she knew a woman who could make me very happy.

I invited both ladies to share a meal with me at my house in the jail's grounds.

Mary was not only a dark-haired woman with bodily curves in the right places and blue eyes which made my heart melt, she was the most caring, loving person I had ever seen. We fell in love and six months later - on January 20, 1956 - exchanged vows at St Mary's, Nassau. It was the foundation for a lifetime of happiness.

I had learnt some valuable lessons before Mary shifted into the house which I had occupied alone in the prison compound.

Before marrying, I never locked the front door of the house. Late one New Year's eve I awakened with a start when my bed suddenly sunk. A big Negro said: "Don't worry, I won't hurt you. It's the governor who I want to kill. Trouble was I didn't pick the time of the change of guards and when I went to get him a guard was with him, so I crept into your house."

The inmate had escaped from the lockup and clearly wanted to get to the governor, whose house was in the compound, rather than try to make his way through the jail's main gate to freedom.

I asked the uninvited man if he would like to help himself to a glass of water and then suggested that he leave. He did, thank God. I then phoned the turnkey and soon the sirens went off and the prisoner was recaptured. He had unknowingly left his

Father Lisle and his wife, Mary, on the wedding day in January, 1956, at St Mary's church, Nassau

Father Lisle looks on as a bride and bridegroom share a cake, a tradition at weddings in the Bahamas

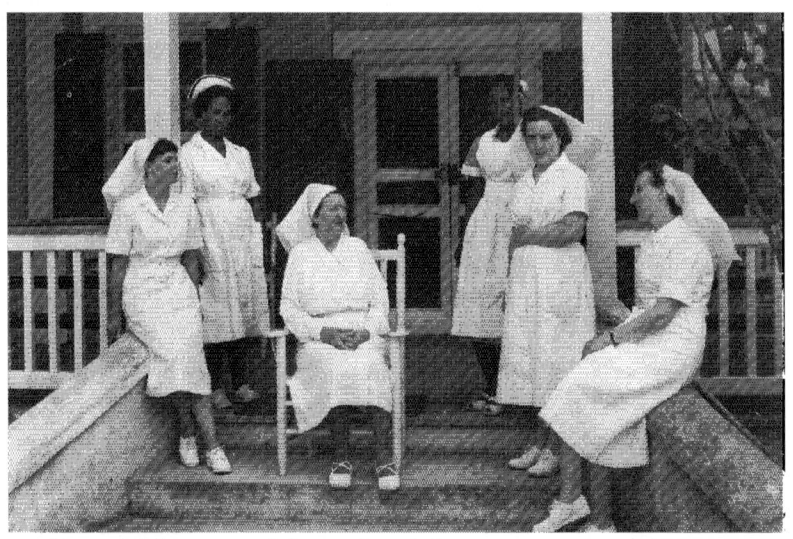

Mary Lisle, second from the right, at a meeting of Nassau nurses. The matron of the hospital is seated.

fingerprints on the glass, giving the authorities evidence that he had been in my home.

Another close-to-home experience involved a trusty prisoner, convicted of murder, who did chores for me.

My house adjoined others for warders and their families, including one warder who had a particularly pretty daughter in her early 20s.

I thought it odd when one day I phoned home from an office which I used in the city to help find former prisoners jobs but the trusty did not answer. Soon afterwards, I opened a cupboard in the spare bedroom and saw scrapings from boots on a wall. They led to the loft in which I found a mattress. My trusty had been engaging in sins of the flesh with the warder's daughter, who was pregnant by the time of my discovery.

The mental instability of prisoners was something I faced regularly, but one confrontation was to be an indelible part of my memory.

I got a phone call one morning from the prison governor who wanted me to take a nail from an inmate who was in the Nassau asylum. The prisoner, who had been transferred to the asylum for treatment, had somehow got hold of the six inch nail and was threatening to harm himself.

When I arrived at the asylum, an officer took me to the man's cell - more like a cage for wild animals. I entered with caution, fearing the prisoner could turn on me without warning or injure himself. The officer stayed outside, as I had asked him to do. "Do you know me?" I asked the prisoner. "Yes, you're Father Lisle from the jail," he replied. The sound of his voice suggested that he had calmed down but I was guarded in case he became agitated again. "I am making something and I need just one nail," I said. "Would you mind giving me a nail?" "Sure Father," he said, and he walked towards me like a lamb holding out the nail for me to take. Once I had it, I glanced towards the cell's door. To my horror, the officer had gone.

I was locked in the cell with the prisoner for much longer than I care to remember before the officer returned. I had the nail but it was terrifying because the inmate could have changed his mind and demanded to be given it back. He was a tough-looking man and I would have had little chance to defend myself if he had grabbed the nail and used it as a weapon.

The women's jail complex also had its fair share of excitement. Female inmates were forced to hand-wash and iron the heavy canvas uniforms worn by their male counterparts as well as do their own laundry. At my insistence, the governor ordered a washing machine to ease their laborious work. The day it arrived, I went with him to the complex to inspect the wash. We found the women had failed to follow the instructions for the big, sputnik-looking machine. Clothes were flying around the laundry and landing in its rafters, the floor was flooded with water and soapsuds and the mess was getting worse by the minute - all because the women had not closed the washer's door.

Female prisoners were far from pampered and, in some instances, deprived of necessities. They had no pads for their monthlies until I convinced the governor to change that prison policy.

Mary didn't like the jail but she wasn't easily frightened. It was also not uncommon for her to help me escort drunks out of street gutters in the city. I had a beautiful wife in every sense and a job that had grown close to my heart. But my close rapport with many of the prisoners was starting to worry me. I was losing my heart to the inmates. If a man escaped and I read in a newspaper that he had been recaptured, I felt sorry for him.

Late in 1956, God gave Mary and me the miracle of a son.

However, there were many anxious moments during many weeks before David was born, especially for Mary who suffered from septicaemia. Mary and I decided it was best for her to return to England because we felt there was likely to be fewer complications with her pregnancy. It was difficult being apart from the woman I loved and having to learn about our son from his mother by phone. It was several months before Mary and David could return home to Nassau. My wife had proved to be incredibly capable in many aspects of life so it came as no surprise when she turned out to be a wonderful mother. I thought I could have been less equipped to be a parent because I lacked a strong father role model when I was a child.

I was born in a hamlet called Hanham, near Bristol, in a manor house, but due to my father's drinking habits we had to shift to a modest home in Bristol. As a two-year-old, I scalded myself with boiling water. My mother, who had been enjoying a peaceful birthday, sent me to get a towel while she was bathing one of my two sisters, Dorothy, who was three years older than I. As I ran through our house I tripped over a fender and fell towards the fire, knocking a saucepan of boiling water over me. The accident restricted me to bed for a year and then I had to learn to walk again.

My father, who was a draper, was an atheist and my mother a Low Church Anglican of sorts. Dorothy, who was called Bobbie, and I and our sister, Gertrude, twelve years my senior, learnt little about God as children.

By the time I turned four, we had moved to another house, in the Welsh town of Bryn Mawr.

One night my mother decided to put me to bed in my upstairs room early so my father could read a newspaper in peace. After she tucked me in, she returned to the room where my father was sitting. He couldn't help but notice from his window a big crowd milling about. "Alice, what are all those people doing outside our house staring up?" he asked. "I don't know Jack but it must be something John is up to," she said.

She returned to my bedroom to find me standing on a chair I had pushed against the room's bay window. I had a towel around me like a surplice and was preaching to passers-by. As my mother put me back to bed I said to her that when I grew up I would be

John Lisle as a boy

John Lisle's mother, Alice Jane Lisle, outside her home in England

a priest, meaning a Catholic priest. Given my lack of knowledge about the role of the clergy, it must have seemed odd to her.

When I was eight I met a High Church Anglican priest who was destined to be my mentor. Father Willfred Jennings was the locum at St Mark's in Gloucester. Father, in his late 20s, had lived and worked in the Bahamas. It is difficult to put in words how I knew that one day I would be ordained a priest but my calling was clear to me and I felt sure Father Jennings was aware of it. I wanted to read the lessons on weekdays at the church so I approached Father. He not only gave me what I wanted but also took me under his wing and we soon became close friends.

About the same time, I was a member of the Gloucester Cathedral Choir, which was giving me confidence and helping me to get the best out of my voice for speaking as well as singing.

I talked with Father Jennings at length about a wide range of subjects. I was fascinated by his experiences as a missionary in the Bahamas. He sometimes talked for hours about the people, their way of life, food and culture, and the challenges faced by Anglican Church clergy in the then British colony.

I later was educated at King's College in London for six years and came under the supervision of the bishop of Gloucester.

When I was ordained a deacon at 24, Father Jennings wrote to me. "Remember the word deacon means a servant and always remember you are a servant of the Church." Those words from the man who had held some sort of hero status for me as a child and whom as an adult I saw as a trusty friend gave me plenty of food for thought. They made me stop and think about my responsibilities as a preacher.

I had few serious concerns about Fox Hill Jail's residents until an inmate threatened to kill my son, a two year old at the time. The inmate, who made the threat after taking a dislike to me, was kept behind bars. The situation was unnerving despite me thinking that the man was unlikely to act on his threat if he got the chance.

Prisoners were supposed to be escorted by guards when they left the jail's main building, such as when they went to work in another part of the compound. But sometimes principles and practices were world's apart.

Father Lisle as a young Anglican priest in Gloucester

One night I returned home from my city office to find prisoners outside the compound. They were wandering in streets and were up lampposts and trees. I stopped my car and asked the guard what was going on.

"A prisoner has escaped and I've sent the others after him," he bellowed.

"Don't be a fool, collect this lot and take them into the prison," I retorted.

My first daughter, Jane, arrived with little fuss for both mother and child in the Nassau hospital where Mary had worked. Unlike David's birth two years earlier, Mary only had to spend a few days in hospital. I thanked God for the healthy birth, not wanting to be apart from my wife for months as we were at the time of our first child.

David and Jane soak up some Nassau sunshine

South African Challenges

About three years after we married, we decided with the Lord's grace, and the help of the Anglican Church, that it was time to move on.

We started our new challenge at Port Elizabeth in South Africa under the auspices of the United Society of the Propagation of the Gospel.

The missionary group supported me to get the post of parish priest of St Francis Xavier, which was in a Chinese community. Bishop Burton commended me to the hierarchy of Grahamstown diocese, which covered Port Elizabeth.

He had written of Mary and me: "His work has been outstandingly fine and I greatly regret that he feels he must give it up ... the diocese of Grahamstown will be fortunate if it secures Father Lisle for either institutional or pastoral work or social service. He has proved in his 10 years in the diocese of Nassau and the Bahamas that he is good at all of these. I can commend his wife in equally high terms. She came to Nassau as a nursing sister at the Princess Margaret Hospital, which is owned and run by the government. After her marriage, she became superintendent of the welfare clinics throughout the colony with all the nurses of that department under her direction."

Many of the people of my new parish were affluent wholesale grocers. I thanked God that most parishioners spoke English because I could not speak a word of their native tongue. I also knew little about their culture, but they lovingly accepted us and the parish was run along Western lines so I coped quite well.

Lack of money was my biggest problem. I was poorly paid

St Francis Xavier at Port Elizabeth, South Africa

Father Lisle with one of many children he baptised at St Francis Xavier, Port Elizabeth

by the missionary society. One time there was no food for the family and Mary became worried. "Don't worry, I'll pray," I said, but she gave me a look that told me she wanted more than prayer. Just at that moment, the front door bell rang. Standing outside was a local grocer, Joseph Ong Hing, holding two big boxes of groceries.

We didn't stay more than a year at the parish because I had long been keen to put my energy into missionary work and a mission south of Port Elizabeth caught my eye. The local archdeacon made sure that I got the job to run the mission based at Humansdorp. It had separate churches and communities for white and black/coloured people as was the policy under apartheid. I travelled many miles to cover it.

South Africa's population in the 1960s comprised about eleven million black people, five million coloured folk and a million whites, who ruled the country under austere racial segregation. At Humansdorp, there were 1000 blacks, 500-600 coloured people and 200 whites. Of course, we lived in the white community - a lot like an English village which had a quaint church and homely rectory in the same grounds.

Blacks and coloureds, the offspring of sexual rendezvous between white men and black women, were on life's poor playing field. They were allowed into my village but had to return to their run-down shacks before night. Blacks and coloureds had to live where they were told to live and do what they were told to do. They were used as labourers, toiling on the likes of farms and roads, and abused by white South Africans.

There were three languages spoken at the mission - English, Afrikaans and Xhosa.

When I said Mass at the black/coloured church of St Patrick outside of Humansdorp village, I did so in all three languages with the help of interpreters. I had been advised by the priest who preceded me to get to know at least one Xhosa term and listen to ensure it was used by the interpreters. Catechists had been known to ignore priests in preference for their own sermons. I decided to take my predecessor's advice and when I heard the interpreters follow suit, I felt confident my sermons were getting to the parishioners.

The black and coloured people openly welcomed me. For them, religion was a source of physical as well as spiritual food. A secret white society collected milk, flour and other foods which were turned into a powder. I used to mix the powder with water in a washing copper and cook the soup in the sacristy. Parishioners brought drinking containers to church and were fed during the service. The people on the Gospel side of the altar drank the soup while those on the Epistle side sang hymns, and later the roles were changed so everyone got a decent feed.

South Africa's secret police followed me to St Patrick but officers never entered. Whether they knew what was going on inside and just chose to ignore it, I'll never know.

Most white people looked down on their dark skinned neighbours and were reluctant to help them. The reaction of a farmer who I asked to donate surplus oranges typified the disdain and cruel attitude which pervaded the nation's white communities. His workers were throwing the oranges into a river because there was a glut on the market.

"Can I stack up my station wagon with your fruit?" I asked.

"Where do you want to take it," he inquired.

I told him that hungry black people at the mission would appreciate the oranges.

"No, you're not getting them," he said angrily. "I'd rather throw them into the river."

Riots were common in South Africa but, thank God, not in or near Humansdorp. Mary and I were forever hearing about lives being wasted by violence.

I will never forget one incident at East London, about 750km from our home, where at least a dozen white campers were decapitated by black people wielding machetes. The whites' caravan was set on fire and as they ran from it to escape the flames, they were beheaded.

On another occasion in the mid 1960s, a white nun who had worked tirelessly for the poor was murdered in a riot at Port Elizabeth. She had spent years caring for sick black and coloured people. When she ventured into a street to see if she could aid the injured, she was killed by rioters. Her death was a reminder to Mary and I that we should not take our safety for granted, even at Humansdorp where the dark community had always embraced us.

The government tried to stay a step ahead of riot organisers by breaking up groups which appeared to have the potential to disrupt the status quo, but the organisers had plenty of devious ways to distribute firearms and disturb the peace. Handguns were sometimes hidden in bread delivered by unsuspecting bread van drivers.

Mary was kept busy at home caring for David and Jane, who were toddlers when we took on the mission challenge, while my days were hectic with priestly duties.

Mary and the children relished the carefree lifestyle and climate, especially the balmy evenings. But my wife and I became troubled parents when David reached school age and attended the local one for young Afrikaners. He was introduced to a world of racist slurs and learnt how to act in an ugly way in the presence of his dark skinned brothers and sisters. The mentality of 'whites are born to rule' surrounded him, misguiding him.

The birth of apartheid has been linked to the Dutch Reformed Church. But, as the story behind the development of apartheid reveals, at least some of the Church's members opposed segregation.

In 1828, the Church Council of Somerset West considered attendance at Holy Communion in terms of race. The council's minutes of March 27, 1828, mentioned a bastard, (assumed over the years to be a coloured man), who wanted to join the congregation. Bentura was baptised but church members did not want him attending Holy Communion with them despite Minister J. Spijker's protestations. Minister Spijker was of the opinion that there should be no discrimination.

Bentura received Holy Communion alongside white people at his baptism on October 26, 1828. This sparked an outcry from white members, who let it be known that should such a thing happen again they would not attend. Most of the members agreed and insisted that the council's decision on strict separation be kept. A number of Scriptures were used to try to justify discrimination. Minister Spijker accused the objectors of having little insight and superficial judgment.

The matter did not rest and an elder reminded him that Saint Paul said if the eating of meat should cause his brother to stumble, then he would never cut it again. The elder argued that if Bentura's presence at Holy Communion caused so much annoyance that people threatened to stay away, then he should refrain from taking part. The elder believed the church council should order him to stay away from the Lord's Supper or to take it separately.

Minister Spijker pointed out the folly of applying what Saint Paul had said. He urged that the next Communion, at Christmas, be free of discrimination. But his call fell on deaf ears and many people were absent from the Communion service.

The Presbytery of Cape Town met in Zwartland on April 29, 1829, and dealt with Somerset West's inquiries on the administering of Communion to black and coloured people. It was asked whether those who had been baptised and confirmed should be allowed to take the Lord's Supper with "born Christians". It was alternatively asked whether for such people it should be obligatory to take Holy Communion separately. The minutes of the meeting do not reveal the discussion but, according to the teachings of the Bible and spirit of Christianity, the churches were reminded that people should take Communion together.

Before the Church Synod meeting in 1829, Minister Spijker

was transferred to Zwartland, where other cases of colour prejudice confronted him. These cases probably contributed to the nature of the proposal that he put to the synod.

But Minister Spijker's proposal was badly edited by the civil department for Church business which left it appearing to oppose open Communion. He was reprimanded by the kommissaris politiek (commissioner of political issues).

The commissioner used his authority as a civil servant to block a question which was humiliating for the Church. He believed that it ought to be an accepted and irrefutable principle that there could be no discrimination at Communion.

Until 1843 the British-run government reserved the right to be involved in Church affairs in such a way that all decisions had to be approved by the civil authority before they could be enforced. The commissioner's task was to ensure that Church meetings were about Church business only. He had the power to prevent topics on agendas from being discussed and could veto decisions.

Synod members from congregations which included Caledon and Stellenbosch, which held segregated Communion services, and Somerset West, which began to follow their example by holding a separate service for Bentura, were not permitted to express their views at the meeting.

One might ask what role Ordinance 50 of 1828 played in deliberations at Church meetings. According to the Ordinance, all free people were considered equal before the law.

In 1831, a community of Khoikhoi was established near Grahamstown. The London Missionary Society initially ministered to these people but the first black congregation, Nederduitse Gereformeerde Kerk, was soon formed. During the next two decades, white people moved to the area and NGK members joined the Stockenstron congregation.

Prejudice became rife and 45 members submitted a petition to the Church Council in 1855. Signatories to the petition wanted a separate congregation within the existing one. They called for the right to choose council members from their own ranks to deal with important matters so that "God's name may not be blasphemed but honoured and praised".

The Church Council rejected the petition.

This did not deter the petition's supporters, who wrote to the council urging that it not be too harsh with their weakness but rather work in the interest of building the congregation. They were of the opinion that to celebrate Communion at two different times of the day would not be contrary to 1Cor.11:33-4 and that by separate celebrations of Communion "both classes of people would be more bound to each other with ties of brotherly love".

The council asked the Presbytery of Albany for advice.

It decided at a meeting in October 1855 to recommend to the council that "in order to meet prejudice and weakness halfway, that after Holy Communion had been administered to the older members of the congregation one or more tables be administered for the new white members".

But the minutes of the presbytery's meeting the following year show the issue had not been resolved.

The synod meeting in 1857 had major reasons to face the tough problem of integrated Holy Communion services. A proposal had been put to the Ceres Church Council that consideration be given to building a separate church where coloured people could be spiritually administered to. The Ceres congregation had been established in 1855 and had favoured segregation from its inception. Minister Shand, the relieving minister from Tulbagh, had turned down this proposal and the council challenged his right to do so.

The synod also had to address Minister Shand's question of whether it was permissible to make a distinction between people at Holy Communion. Since the 1820s it had been said that any discrimination at Communion was not allowed but in practice there was discrimination.

The synod's decision reads: "The synod considers it desirable and according to the Holy Scripture that our heathen members be accepted and initiated into our congregations wherever it is possible. But where this measure, as a result of the weakness of some, stands in the way of promoting the work of Christ among the heathen then congregations set up among the heathen, or still to be set up, should enjoy their Christian privileges in a separate building or institution."

The synod declared that according to the Bible, it was clear that differences between race should not cause any difference to be made in the preaching of the Gospel. But it also acknowledged that there was strong prejudice among some white people.

This predisposition of a section of the Church, which came to be called a weakness, was tolerated. It led to the Church losing any impression that it was against colour discrimination.

The Ugly Politics Behind Apartheid

I think the belief that apartheid could be theologically justified was not the prime mover - political ideology was at the forefront of the system which sought to subjugate black and coloured people. Moreover, selfish South African white people, especially the nation's leaders, saw division as a means of furthering their own ends.

It has been argued that the origins of racially-divided South Africa can be traced to closely linked factors, namely the racial division of labour and capitalism, responses to militant struggles waged by white labour, immigration policy and a so-called poor white problem.

With the discovery of diamonds at Kimberley and gold in the Transvaal, thousands of people, most of them from England, streamed to South Africa. There were more than 50,000 migrants in Kimberley by the early 1870s. People from many different walks of life had decided to seek riches in South Africa. There were many problems due to the migration. Workers needed economic, social and psychological security.

In the tumult of the time, unionists began to occupy themselves in organising and implementing strategies designed to relieve the suffering of migrant workers. These unions were largely craft unions formed by skilled white people and only open to white workers in certain trades. They defended their members' monopoly right to do certain tasks.

The unions adopted racially discriminatory membership rules.

Mine chiefs tried to reorganise a number of labour processes done by skilled white workers so they would be done by groups of workers, including blacks. There were large-scale strikes over the issue. The basic demand was for the imposition or restoration of job colour bars.

The fundamental notion of universal socialism was scrapped as the South African Labour Party saw itself as the protector of white labour against coloured competition and capitalism.

Labour's Patrick Duncan argued that everyone would agree with the principle that it was in the best interests of Europeans and blacks that points of social contact should be reduced to the least possible area (Debates, House of Assembly, 1913).

South Africa Party leader Jannie Smuts, who was asked what the government was doing to address the labour unrest, told the Imperial war cabinet in London: "We have realised that political ideas which apply to our white civilisation largely do not apply to the administration of native affairs. To apply the same institutions on equal basis to black and white alike does not lead to the best results. We have legislation before the Parliament to create all over South Africa, wherever there are any considerable native communities, independent self-governing institutions for them."

Some people felt that South Africa's political leaders should be careful not to allow the unions to prescribe how to govern. They argued that another possibility would be to look at the immigration policy. The argument was that European migrants did not understand the South African context and were not willing to accept that black people could not just be barred from jobs to please migrants. Migrants were adamant to fight on for rights as they competed with blacks for labour. Often management preferred to employ blacks because they were paid less.

The capitalists' attitude led to the poor white problem.

The number of poor whites reached 106,518, about 8 per cent of the white population, by 1916 and more than 300,000, 17.5 per cent, by 1932. This concerned some capitalists and the State was urged to ensure the assignment of white people rather than blacks to some jobs.

A series of mine strikes on the Witwatersrand preceded an ugly historical event in 1922. It was called the Witwatersrand Miners' Strike, or the Red Revolt. White workers were infuriated at the prospect of wage reductions and losing their jobs to black people. About 22,000 white mine workers united under South African Communist Party leaders. Most of the men believed they were fighting for the rights of white miners. More than 230 people were killed, 5000 were arrested, 1400 prosecuted and 864 convicted. Four were hanged. The strikers achieved their objective- to keep labour in South Africa segregated.

With the National Party winning office in 1948, the Dutch Reformed Church said: "As a Church, we have always worked purposefully for the separation of races. In this regard, apartheid can rightfully be called a Church policy."

Up to this assertion, the Church did not have an official policy on apartheid.

In 1974, the Church cautiously warned in its publication Ras, volk en nasie, (Race, People and Nation), that Christians must be careful not to change natural diversity into sinful separateness. In October 1986, the Church condemned those forms of apartheid that "could lead to a system where certain groups could be favoured above others". But it was not an admission that all forms of apartheid were wrong.

The revised edition of Kerk en Samelewing, (Church and Society), approved by the synod in October 1990, said: "Any form of racism is a grievous sin that no man or Church can or must defend or practice."

The Church had rejected racism in all forms as contradictory to the word of God.

Some people have mistakenly associated the Reformed Churches of Australia with the Dutch Reformed Church. The first Reformed Churches of Australia set up in 1951. It is significant that members opted for the Reformed Churches name, not for it to be known as a Dutch Reformed Church. The only link this Church has with the Dutch Reformed Church of South Africa is that of heritage. They have their roots in the Reformed Churches of the Netherlands.

With the Reformed Churches in the Netherlands, the Reformed Churches of Australia condemned the Dutch Reformed Church for its justification of apartheid.

During my six years at Humansdorp mission, the big number of converts to the Dutch Church dumbfounded me.

Many laws made by the government of the day riled me - they were designed to keep white people as top dogs. For example, my understanding of one Act was that it allowed whites to assume control of land and property occupied by blacks and coloureds. Whites would take over houses, buildings and land when and where they wanted, displacing black and coloured people without compensation.

Under another law, it seemed a black man could be executed almost at the drop of a hat if he had a relationship with a white woman. It was my understanding that this Act was set up to stop crossbreeding.

Education and health for black South Africans were low on the government's list of priorities. My understanding of one education Act was that it meant black and coloured children were not permitted English lessons and were not required to attend school. Discouraging their education was a way of keeping blacks/coloureds under the whites' control.

Black hospitals were overcrowded, lacked medicines and basic foods and often were even short of bandages. Black ambulances were run-down and, of course, white ambulances were for whites only. White ambulance officers would not pick up a black person dying beside a road.

How South Africa progressed from the 1960s to the democracy of today without more blood being shed may have something to do with the nature of the country's dark people. I was a resident at a disturbing time but, unlike many other people with white skin, could see most of my dark neighbours had great potential to forgive. A lot of white races have shown far less tolerance to adversities throughout the Ages.

I found it impossible to turn the other cheek to apartheid and vehemently preached against it in Humansdorp's big white church, St Mark's. One morning while leaving home, I noticed some linesmen working on adjacent phone lines.

"Good morning, I guess you men are tapping our phone?" I asked, tongue-in-cheek.

There was no response.

After that, whenever I picked up the phone and dialled, I heard a click and suspected the secret police were monitoring my moves. I felt that I was at risk of being arrested for treason.

No single Church or organisation was in a position to force much needed changes to the status quo. I knew that change would be slow.

The Anglican Church opposed the government over apartheid policies, but unfortunately the same could not be said for the majority of Catholic leaders. Most Catholics sat on the fence, steering clear of any public stand against apartheid policies. A number of Anglican bishops have been recorded in history books for their courage. Some of them died in exile after being deported for taking a stand against apartheid.

The whites' right to rule was ingrained and it was easy for even the most devout Christians to lose the plot. One day when I was ill I arranged for a priest from Port Elizabeth to celebrate the Eucharist for the mission's white people and arranged for a coloured lad to be an altar boy. Shortly before Mass, the church warden left St Mark's, complaining that he had a stomach-ache. The truth was that he wanted an excuse to leave because the boy was inside.

The privilege of being born white meant having the most modern comforts of the day and household servants to tend to your every need. But I got some timely reminders of the inequality, such as one morning after Mass in the black church when I thoughtlessly told my catechist how I was looking forward to a hearty breakfast. "Good luck to you Father, most of your parishioners have no breakfast to go home to," he remarked.

I helped my less fortunate parishioners in whatever ways I could. I think being a white priest was advantageous in that I would have been more able than a black priest to get donations of foodstuffs and medicines. And in a novel event, I was welcomed as a worker alongside coloured people to build a mud brick church, St Mary the Virgin, near Humansdorp village. But it probably would have been too much to expect to be regarded as a bosom buddy because being white meant I was reminder of the people who tormented them.

While teaching a black and coloured Confirmation class one day, a strapping youth turned to me and asked: "Father, how long do you think a million white people can keep eleven million black people down?" Peter, 17, was obviously desperate for change, and I could not argue with him. He was being used as an errand boy when in most Western nations he would have got much more suitable employment opportunities.

My church and rectory gardener, Joseph, became the closest black man in my life. Joseph was paid two pounds to work a seven-day week. Needless to say, he was being unfairly compensated for his toil. I could have spoken out against it but I knew there was nothing that could be accomplished other than getting him the sack. But he must have realised that I cared because years later, when my time came to leave the mission, he knelt at my feet and said: "Father, always remain the man you are now."

Apartheid also strained relationships with fellow white people because they found it impossible to understand how I became immersed in my work for black and coloured people. I knew that if I attacked apartheid too much outside church, most white people would not listen and would not talk to me. Somehow I had to tread a fine line to do my work as a priest. Even the friendship I struck up with Douglas Lowrens, a parishioner with whom I had much in common, had limits. Douglas was a hard working farmer and a strong family man. He was a good mate to have in a tough country, but sometimes our conversations were hindered by apartheid policies and attitudes. It was impossible to be frank with each other at all times.

Mary would have liked to have had more time to care for Humansdorp's dark people. As a mother of young children, her time was limited - especially after the arrival of our second daughter, Mary, who was born at a Blue Sisters-run hospital at Port Elizabeth in 1960, the third miracle of my union with her beautiful mother.

My wife's compassion for blacks was evident through the time she set aside to make pots of soup on her wooden stove for them. Joseph spread the word and she was inundated by hungry black people at her soup servings outside our back door. It seemed the danger of being caught and penalised by law enforcers was far from her mind.

She had no hesitation caring for a black priest who became ill with tuberculosis even though such kindness could have got her into all sorts of trouble with the authorities. She drew the curtains in our home as she nursed him back to health.

Mary's midwifery skills came to the fore during a holiday in Cape Town with our young maid. I couldn't afford to pay for accommodation so we arranged the holiday on the basis that I would be locum at a parish, saying Mass and helping to solve any big problems that arose. Of course, our dark skinned maid had to sleep in quarters outside the main house because it was illegal for her to do otherwise.

One day I had a stomach-ache and decided to postpone a family picnic. As I rested on a bed in the rectory, an elderly lady who lived with us, called Grandma Brown, rushed into the room holding a pair of scissors. "What are you going to do with those?" I asked. "It's the maid, she's having a baby Father," Grandma replied.

I was shocked because the maid had not been showing as

A service starts at St Mark's in Humansdorp

Grandma Brown with David and Jane

Father Lisle outside St Mark's at Humansdorp

one would expect of a near full-term pregnant woman. Mary and I suspected the father was a policeman. It was common for members of the constabulary to arrest black women and seek sexual favours on promises of release without charges. When we returned home, I appealed to my white parishioners for clothes for the girl. They were generous, which was not surprising because they had often showed generosity as long as black and coloured people were kept at a distance.

The white rights which came with apartheid were something my parishioners had taken in with their mother's milk. I tried to get my anti-apartheid message across in subtle ways, such as through a prayer offered at the start of almost every Mass.

God our Father, You guide everything in wisdom and love. Accept the prayers we offer for our nation.

By the wisdom of our leaders and the integrity of our citizens, may harmony and justice be secured and may there be lasting prosperity and peace.

We ask this through our Lord Jesus Christ your son who lives and reigns with You and with the Holy Spirit.

One God for ever and ever. Amen.

I had a lot to be grateful for - being born white yet able to see the evil behind apartheid. I also had a wonderful woman who nurtured our children and supported me in my vocation and through times of great grief, such as when my mother died shortly after Mary and I married.

In the mid 1960s, when I was 40-something and suffering from prostate problems exasperated by countless hours driving at the mission, we agreed it was time to move on.

Our new parish was the all-whites St Mark's in the southern port city of East London, between Port Elizabeth and Durban. One of the first people I met after we arrived was the priest from the neighbouring Anglican parish.

"You mustn't be upset if people pass your church door on Sunday morning to go to mine Father," he said.

Tongue-in-cheek, I replied: "It might happen the other way around."

As it turned out, that's precisely what happened, despite my being unwell more often than not and unable to work tirelessly like I did at Humansdorp.

St Mark's was soon packed with about 300 parishioners regularly attending Sunday Mass, compared with 50 when I started the job. My Church colleague's numbers became thinner and thinner. He had misjudged my rapport with the parishioners - a lot of which I put down to the music I introduced for Mass. I struck a chord with them through perennials like All Things Bright and Beautiful and The Office Hymn for Vespers.

My family and I settled surprisingly well at St Mark's. I initially had not been keen on going to the parish because my heart was set on a blooming parish in Cape Town.

I was blessed by a reunion with Father John Matthews, who was based at Johannesburg but made the long journey to visit and concelebrate Mass with me. Father Matthews and I had much in common and we seemed to be walking on a similar path as Christian leaders.

Bishop of Grahamstown Gordon Tyndale did not share my papal Anglican views but he was delighted that I succeeded in boosting the St Mark's flock. I managed to change the High Church I inherited towards an Anglo-Catholic way of worship, picking up new parishioners without upsetting the long-timers.

I think people knew that despite my prostate-related and other health problems, I loved serving the Lord and His people. And when they went to Mass, they knew that I would call things as I truly saw them, apartheid included. I was sure that most of my parishioners were pro-apartheid.

One day I learnt that the black man who cleaned the church was coughing vigorously and often so I left the intercom between

Father Lisle greets parishioners after a Mass at St Mark's, East London

A service at St Mark's, East London. Father John Matthews is concelebrating with Father Lisle

the church and the rectory on so I could monitor him. I told the church's two wardens of my concern that he might have tuberculosis, but they told me that he was putting it on. Nothing was done to help him until it was too late - he died. He would not have been left to fend for himself if he'd been born white.

Call to Become Catholics

England

We were only at St Mark's for about a year when we decided I should resign to return to England. Mary was worried about my ailing health and we thought it best that we live in England where a Harley Street specialist could treat me.

When I tendered my resignation to Bishop Tyndale in October 1964, he said he was saddened to lose my services and wrote in my commendation:

"There are two noteworthy facets of his character. One is that he is a man of prayer. The other is that he has a great love of people. I do not believe that I have met another man who has a keener pastoral sense. He loves and is loved, and his goodness shines out of him ... He teaches rather than preaches. He leads and does not drive. He so inspires people that acts of worship conducted by him lifts them into an atmosphere of holiness."

Archbishop of Cape Town Robert Taylor, who was Bishop Tyndale's predecessor in Grahamstown, also wrote kindly of me. "I worked closely with him. He served most faithfully a country parish with a very large number of outstations, and proved himself to be a good teacher and tireless worker."

Father Superior of St Cuthbert's, Alan Young, who had seen much of my work at Humansdorp, wrote: "His years in that very difficult job were years of very hard work but it must have been a great joy to him to have been allowed to see his labours so wonderfully rewarded. In this country of stress and strain, he made his parish church a true home with a real family spirit, and then he was able to teach the people the faith."

The next challenge put my way by the United Society missionary group was to work from Leeds as secretary of the propagation of the gospel. Like a number of priests, I was required to visit parishes to preach and raise money for overseas projects. It was a task which gave me new spark in my life.

I had only been in the job a short time when the bishop of Lincoln phoned and asked me to meet him. He did not say why he wanted to talk to me. Mary stayed in a Lincoln restaurant while I went to visit the bishop. I was flabbergasted by his plan to move me to one of his best parishes and provide the sort of accommodation most priests dream of.

"But you don't know anything about me," I said. We had not met before that day.

"You've been a missionary all your life and that's all I need to know about you," he said.

He wanted me for the job because he knew that as a missionary, I was full of fervour when preaching the gospel. He was bitterly disappointed when I told him that I was not interested in the position because Mary and I had other plans, which included shifting to Australia.

My health had improved but Mary was frightfully chesty in the cold English climate and doctors suggested that she would be better off in a warmer country. We didn't want to return to South Africa because of its apartheid but knew we would not stay long in England.

We talked with our children about moving, in line with our policy to involve them in as many family matters as was practical. David and Jane were in lower primary school and Mary was approaching school age. The family decision was made easier by an extraordinary event. While we slept in our bedrooms one night part of the dining room ceiling fell to the floor. The shape left in the ceiling by the cave-in was that of a near perfect map of Australia. You can imagine our reaction when we woke from our slumber and saw what had happened.

David, Jane and Mary as young children in England

Mary and I had discussed the pros and cons of converting to the Roman Catholic faith for many years. I probably had leanings that way when flying the papal flag on the boat Gordon and I relied on so much in the Bahamas. There had been obstacles holding me back, including that there were no married priests in the Catholic Church's Latin Rite, or at least none that I knew of, and it seemed to me that I would have poor prospects of changing the status quo. Married priests had been unheard of since the 10th century.

The older I became the more I was disillusioned as an Anglican. But I felt powerless to free myself from the trap which held me, from the shackles which were preventing me fulfil my vocation in life as a Catholic. I was sure the Anglican hierarchy would howl me down and that Catholic leaders would not accept me as a Catholic priest.

We had been back in England for about a year when we decided to shift to Australia. I then wrote to Anglican Archbishop of Perth George Appleton and met him when he visited London. He said he had nowhere in his archdiocese for me but that the Bishop of Bunbury, Ralph Hawkins, might be able to find a parish for me. I took Archbishop Appleton's advice and contacted the Bishop, who offered me the post of parish priest of Mt Barker.

At Southampton, Mary and I met the Catholic chaplain of the liner which was to take us to WA. Some people might think it was a chance meeting but I'm sure it was brought about by the hand of God because the course of my life was changed.

I told the chaplain, Father Gregory Manley, that we were yearning to become Catholics. He asked where we were going to live in Australia. When I replied that Mt Barker was going to be my new parish, he smiled and said: "You couldn't be going anywhere better. You're going to be in the Bunbury diocese of Bishop Launcelot Goody and if any bishop will do anything for you, he will."

Father Manley's words gave me the encouragement and hope that I desperately needed. As simple as they were, they opened a door in my mind which had been shut and bolted all of my life.

Mount Barker

We got a warm welcome at Mt Barker. The parishioners had furnished our new home and had cooked us a hearty meal. They had even made our beds. We thanked God because we had next to nothing and it had been a long, tiring journey from England.

Bishop Hawkins shared my Anglo-Catholic background, which made my start at Mt Barker a lot easier than it might have been - especially when I insisted on being called Father Lisle by parishioners who were used to the informality of my predecessor. The Bishop could empathise with his 50-year-old recruit but if he had been in my position he might have been more subtle than I was.

The local Catholic priest, Father Jim McCarthy, attended

my induction as rector which I was delighted about. I had been keen to meet him because I thought we might talk on another occasion about my desire to join the Catholic Church.

A few days later, I called on him.

When I told him that Mary and I were determined to be Catholics, he was staggered. I thought his reaction was somewhat surprising because he knew that I insisted on being called Father. He sent me to Monsignor Charles Cunningham, who was based in nearby Albany. I promptly made my way to the port town, only to find that Monsignor Cunningham referred me to Bishop Goody.

I decided my best opportunity to discuss the matter with the Bishop was by inviting him to dinner after a Confirmation in Mt Barker.

"I want to become a Catholic," I told him in the quiet of the family lounge room after the meal.

"You'd want to go on doing what you're doing now wouldn't you?" he asked.

"Good gracious, yes I do if it is possible," I replied.

"I shall make it possible," he declared.

I was flabbergasted. I did not know of any other move in the world for a married Anglican to covert to Catholicism and the Bishop knew little about me and my family. We had only been in WA for a few months.

I had thought I would have to look for a job because my chosen Church would never accept me as one of its priests, especially after I had been an Anglican priest for more than twenty five years. But Bishop Goody was steady in the face of obvious obstacles and prepared to help me continue my vocation in the Catholic Church. The Bishop had incredible nerve considering the last time the Church had widely entertained married priests was before the celibacy rule was introduced in the 10th century.

Saint Peter, the first Pope, was married as were many of the apostles. But the Church decided celibacy was a better policy so clergy would have more time for pastoral work. The policy enabled a priest to be a member of every family in his parish.

Saint Paul, the apostle, said a married man could not give all his time to God because he had to please a wife. I think a married priest's wife must be a special kind of woman for both their sakes because she has to take second place in his life.

The celibacy rule is Church made, it is not a Divine law, and as such can be changed, but I believe most Catholic priests and their parishioners support it.

Mary and I felt ready to become Catholics as soon as was practical.

I knew that at last we would be in communion with the Pope for our salvation. The Holy Father is the centre of unity. There was nothing Anglican about me and I should not have been in the Church. It would be affirmed time and again after we became Catholics that we had made the right decision.

The Anglican Church was on the wrong track when, in later years, it backed the ordination of women. The Lord Jesus did not call women to be priests though some of the women who knew him were the most faithful of servants.

Why didn't Jesus ordain Our Mother Mary or Martha?

Thank God Pope John Paul, whom I met in Western Australia in later years, has condemned any move for women priests in the Catholic Church.

The motley crowd in the Anglican Church - High Church, Low Church and a number of shades in between - have passed all sorts of controversial laws in recent years. Lay people can even celebrate the Eucharist in some churches.

About six months after Bishop Goody gave me his support, I received dispensation from the Vatican to become a priest of the Catholic Church's Latin Rite.

In the meantime, I had my silver jubilee as an Anglican priest without going public on my decision to leave the Church.

Before I made public my intention to leave, I wanted to

Launcelot Goody, as Bishop of Bunbury, helped Father Lisle in his move from the Anglican to Catholic Church.

discuss the merits of Catholicism with two married Anglican priests because I felt they might join me. Fathers Frederick "Geoff" Beyer and Rodney Williams were tending to parishes in the diocese of Bunbury. I was sure they were more interested in Rome than they let on. I invited Father Beyer, a married man in his 30s with four children, to visit me.

"What do you think of the Roman Church?" I asked.

"I haven't really thought about it Father," he answered.

"You're telling me that you haven't thought about joining it?" I persisted.

"Oh, no," he said.

I could see that my questions had put him on the back foot so I decided not to pressure him. There was no point in embarrassing him. I told him that I was joining the Church and that if he was ever interested, I would talk to Bishop Goody on his behalf. Later, I confronted Father Williams, who was in his mid 40s with two children, only to get a similar reaction.

Shortly before I intended to announce my decision to become a Catholic, a missionary visited the Mt Barker parish to speak at a Sunday service. The church was full to the brim. After Mass, I strolled towards a newsagency in the town's sleepy but pleasant retail centre. I got a rude awakening as I approached - a poster read that an Anglican cleric had been named for Rome.

The Sunday Times had my story in graphic detail on its front page - the biggest move of my life, which I was more than a little keen to keep secret from WA's senior Anglicans, had been let out of the bag. The Holy See had released information about my conversion unbeknown that I had not approached the Anglican hierarchy to resign, let alone been received to be a Catholic deacon. It was then 1968, West Australians were conservative and an Englishman with three children was to be one of the first married priests in the Catholic Church's Latin Rite for hundreds of years.

There were more shocks, two in fact, in store. Fathers Beyer and Williams plucked up the courage to join me on what we thought would be a bumpy road towards the Catholic Church. I had faced many challenges over the years but I was less sure about how to handle the Anglican hierarchy than deal with politicians like industrial development minister Charles Court.

I hit out at Mr Court, who was to become one of the State's most prominent premiers, over his approach to South Africa. In January 1967, Mr Court praised South Africa's treatment of coloured people. During a visit to the country, he said many critics of its regime were fanatical. As The Daily News reported, I described the statement as pathetic and said the minister was out of step with the majority of Christian thinking on South Africa.

Bishop Hawkins wasted no time sending for me when he learnt of my intention to join the Catholics. Sitting on his rostrum, he looked at me sternly.

"I think you're the ringleader. You ought to know better," he said. "You're a senior priest who has disturbed the other two priests. If you stay in the Anglican Church, you will leave Mt Barker, come on the staff of the cathedral, you'll work under my strict supervision and you'll have nothing to do with Roman Catholics. Do you accept that Father?"

I replied: "My Lord, if I was staying in the Anglican Church I would, but I'm not."

He was taken aback. Then, when he regained composure, he graciously asked to give me a blessing. I left after the blessing and went to pick up Mary from Bishop Goody's. He was welcoming and, like me, pleased that life as an Anglican was behind me.

But Mary and I were to face enormous upheaval over the next few months before being received formally by WA's Catholics.

We were given three days to vacate the Mt Barker rectory.

I had succeeded in boosting the numbers of parishioners and was saddened by the sudden eviction. Molly Chapman, who worked at the local Aboriginal mission with her husband, Bert, was to tell me in later years:

The Aboriginal mission near Mt Barker kept Molly and Bert Chapman and friends busy

"They all loved your sermons Father. Even the people who didn't like you much went to church to hear you preach."

I used to walk up and down the church's aisles, stopping regularly without notice to question people about what I was preaching about. It was a style of preaching I had never employed before taking up the post at Mt Barker parish but, as Mrs Chapman noted, it seemed to work. The people who went to All Saints Church were kept on their toes - they dared not fall asleep on the pews. The church was so packed most Sundays that I had to find more chairs from somewhere else. Before he learnt of my move to become a Catholic, Bishop Hawkins told me that he thought a bigger church would have to be built.

After I left the Anglican priesthood eight of my former Mt Barker parishioners converted to Catholicism. None of them was close to me but I couldn't help but wonder if my decision to become a Catholic had started them thinking seriously about their faith. While I was well on the way to joining the Catholics I had

had a visit from a woman who told me: "I've got some bad news for you Father, I'm becoming a Catholic."

My rescript from the Vatican to be a married Catholic priest was in a closed tin box near where she was sitting in my office. I wanted to tell her that both of us would soon be Catholics but I was not ready to make my move public so I thought it best to keep my own counsel. I could only wish her well and let her go on thinking that I was a pillar of the Anglican Church.

Faced with eviction and with nowhere to go, I asked Monsignor Cunningham for help. He was only able to offer us temporary accommodation in a caravan at Albany. Mary cried most of the first night - it would have been a trying time for any mother with three young children.

A few weeks later, we moved to Perth, but our new home was very ordinary. The Catholic Church helped us to find a house in Mt Lawley which was more suitable for a family. But it was not long before we had to shift again because the house had been used as a drop-in by delinquents and Mary and I feared for the safety of the children when all sorts turned up on our doorstep.

Mary went back to work as a nurse because I did not have a parish and, therefore, was without an income. She got a job at what was then St Anne's Mercy Hospital, Mt Lawley, and I took on her household duties such as the washing and cleaning.

We were destined to live in the Scarborough parish where I was to start my vocation with the Church as a deacon.

First Married Catholic Priests

It was on May 25, 1969, that Fathers Williams and Beyer joined me at St Mary's Cathedral, Perth, to be ordained deacon.

In October, we were ordained priests by newly appointed Archbishop Goody. The West Australian newspaper splashed news of both events across its front page.

My ordination to the Catholic priesthood was one of the happiest days of my life but, of course, few Anglicans attended. Mary and I had not lived in WA long enough to form many close friendships, the sort that endure thick and thin.

As our loved ones and friends proudly looked on, Archbishop

Three of a kind - Fathers Geoff Beyer, left, John Lisle and Rodney Williams made the brave move from the Anglican to Catholic Church

The West Australian

ESTABLISHED 1833 — PERTH SATURDAY MAY 24 1969 — 88 PAGES 5c

Former parsons to be R.C. priests

Three former Anglican priests—all married—will be ordained deacons in St. Mary's Roman Catholic Cathedral tomorrow. They will be the first three married men ordained Roman Catholic deacons in W.A.

John Lisle, Rodney Williams and Frederick Beyer will be ordained by the Roman Catholic Archbishop of Perth, the Most Rev. Dr L. J. Goody.

After further studies the three men will be ordained priests late this year.

Till recently married men were not admitted as deacons or priests into the Roman Catholic church.

However, since the second Vatican council of 1962 the custom has been growing.

A deacon cannot celebrate Mass nor hear confessions but he can conduct baptisms, weddings and funerals, assist at Holy Communion, and can instruct people in the faith.

The three men will live with their families after their ordination tomorrow and will carry out the parish duties of a deacon.

It is normally the custom for a single man who becomes a deacon to return to college for studies in the period between his ordination as deacon and his ordination as priest.

Yesterday the three men were in retreat in preparation for their ordination.

Mr Beyer and Mr Lisle were formerly Anglican ministers in the Bunbury diocese. Mr Williams was formerly rector of Cranbrook, in the Great Southern.

In March, last year, Mr Beyer and Mr Lisle received a special papal dispensation through the Roman Catholic doctrinal congregation relieving them of the chastity vow normally required of Roman Catholic priests.

Mr Beyer, who has four children and is in his mid-thirties, resigned from the Anglican ministry in January last year. He has since been teaching science, mathematics and French at the St. Louis School, Claremont. He was educated at Scotch College and is a science graduate of the W.A. University. He was a teacher before he entered the Anglican ministry.

Mr Williams, who is in his forties and has two children, resigned from the Anglican ministry in December, 1967. He has been working in a lay capacity at St. John of God Hospital, Subiaco.

Change for three priests

The first people to receive communion from these three newly-ordained Roman Catholic priests yesterday were their wives and children. The men were formerly Anglican ministers.

The Rev. Frederick Geoffrey Beyer, who has four children, the Rev. John Edward Lisle (three children) and the Rev. Rodney John Williams (two children) each gave communion.

More than 1,000 people watched the Roman Catholic Archbishop of Perth, the Most Rev. Dr L. J. Goody, perform the first Roman Catholic ordination of married men in W.A.

The men became Roman Catholics last year.

Dr Goody told the congregation that they had received special papal dispensation which exempted them from the usual vows of celibacy.

Father P. G. V. O'Reilly, secretary to the Archbishop said that one of the problems that faced the new priests was the education of their children.

The Church would pay for this.

It is expected that Father Lisle will be re-assigned to the Scarborough parish where he has been working as a deacon.

Father Williams may be appointed to the Applecross parish.

Father Lisle

Goody officiated in the laying on of hands and then anointed our hands with oil and gave us the gifts, a pattern with a Host and a chalice containing wine.

Monsignor Cunningham and the parish priest of Mt Barker were among the clergy who joined the Archbishop and his three new priests to offer the bread and wine for it to be changed into the body and blood of Christ in Holy Communion.

The media swarmed around after the Mass and the ugly side of their business soon became apparent. Mary and I were hounded for days by reporters who parked themselves outside the front of our home. We used the house's back door in a bid to get some privacy. Their persistence made us feel like prisoners in our own home.

"What made you do it? Why did you do it?"

"How long are you going to stay?" - the questions rang out as the reporters sought to get stories.

My reason for joining the Church was to be in communion with the Pope but I'm sure some people will never believe me.

The story of my change in allegiance from Anglican to Catholic was picked up by media all over the world. One illustration sent to me by a friend living in England was to remain clear in my memory for many years. It is a pity the name of the provincial publication which ran the cartoon escapes my mind because credit should be given where credit is due. The cartoon was of a priest putting nappies on a clothes line.

The caption read: "Our dad has become a Father."

My friend told me the cartoon ran in a publication in the Bristol area, where I had spent part of my childhood. I would laugh heartily each time it came to mind.

The fact that I preferred to be called Father when I was a married Anglican priest did not detract from the creative yet simplified approach to an event which not only changed my life but set a precedent in the Catholic Church. In future years, there were to be more married Anglicans accepted into the Catholic

Church as priests. Some were to be prompted towards Catholicism for wider reasons than mine.

The emergence of women priests in the Anglican Church could be seen as activating the switch of allegiance for many married men in England and in the United States. In 1994, Father William Saunders outlined some of the US changes in the paper in which he had a regular column, the Arlington Catholic Herald, Texas. Father Saunders was appointed founding pastor of Our Lady of Hope Parish in Potomac Falls while remaining dean of the Notre Dame Graduate School of Christendom College. Father Saunders told how the Episcopal (Anglican) Church faced internal turmoil in the mid 1970s. Women were ordained as priests in 1976 and in later years ordained as bishops.

In 1979, the Episcopalians revised Thomas Cranmer's Book of Common Prayer. They used contemporary language and added various liturgical options to the first Protestant Archbishop of Canterbury's service book.

More recently, there had been support among some people in the Church for the ordination of homosexuals and for homosexual marriages.

This support, which Father Saunders referred to in 1994, was more than that by 1997. In the US, Bishop Frank Griswold, who openly endorsed gay sex, was appointed primate. In the United Kingdom, a number of bishops gave qualified approval to gay sex. The Bishop of Jarrow, Dr Alan Smithson, said he was willing to bless "gay unions" (marriages).

Of course, there were clergy against these moves. At a meeting of Anglicans, which included bishops and archbishops, held in Kuala Lumpur it was agreed that such actions called into question Holy Scriptures and were totally unacceptable. Father Saunders made the point in the Arlington Herald in 1994 that it was change which prompted a number of Episcopalian clergy and laity to convert to Catholicism. The Catholic priest said most of these converts had been High-Episcopalians.

Pope John Paul, through the Sacred Congregation for the Doctrine of the Faith, had issued a statement in 1980 to help priests and other Anglicans wanting to become Catholics. He said about married Episcopalian clergy becoming Catholic priests of the Latin Rite: "The Holy See has specified that this exception to the rule of celibacy is granted in favour of these individuals, and should not be understood as implying any change in the Church's conviction of the value of priestly celibacy."

In other words, an Episcopalian priest could make a profession of faith and be received into the Catholic Church, and thereupon receive the sacrament of Confirmation. He would then take appropriate courses which would enable him to minister as a Catholic priest. After proper examination by his bishop and with the Holy Father's permission, he would be ordained first as a Catholic transitional deacon and later as a priest.

If the former Episcopalian was unmarried at the time of his ordination, he would take the vow of celibacy. If the ex-Anglican was married, he would be exempt from making the celibacy promise. However, if he became a widower he would be bound to the celibate lifestyle.

The Pope also provided Episcopalians wanting to convert to Catholicism with the option of "a common identity reflecting certain elements of their own heritage". This "pastoral provision" enabled a congregation to enter the Catholic Church and be allowed to remain a parish. The congregation could use an Anglican-style Catholic Mass with either the traditional Book of Common Prayer or the modern English version. Of course, Episcopalian laity could convert to Catholicism as individuals if they preferred.

St Mary the Virgin Episcopal Church in Arlington became St Mary the Virgin Catholic Church in 1994. Father Allan Hawkins, married with two children, and a congregation of 120 people converted with the help of the Holy Father's pastoral provision. Father Hawkins, an Anglican priest of more than 30 years, recounted the story to the Catholic Answer Live radio network.

Father said the ordination of women as priests and the Episcopal Church's softening on a range of moral issues were catalysts in the conversion. But the underlying reason his parishioners wanted to make the change had more to do with their belief that they should be in unity - the sort of unity only available in the Church headed by the Pope.

Father Hawkins explained that the Anglican Church occupied a position between the hard-core breakaway Protestant Churches formed out of the Reformation in the 16th century and the Catholic Church. In fact, the Anglican High Church position in many ways was essentially Catholic.

He said challenges and changes which he and his Episcopalian parishioners faced, Church issues which they found themselves constantly grappling with, were seen as weakening authority.

Scripture and tradition, which Episcopalians had relied on for authority for hundreds of years, were under threat.

His parish community agreed that there was desperate need for stability - which they later found in communion with the Holy Father.

Father Hawkins said he had made it clear to his parishioners that he had been interested in converting for many years. When he arrived at the parish from England in the 1980s he had tried to set out the major issues facing Episcopalians in a fair and open way. It was not until the congregation met in 1991 to review the latest general convention of the Episcopal Church that the "right time" arrived for the conversion to take shape. Father told radio listeners that his parishioners were agitated by the way the Episcopal Church was splitting.

The spark started an emotional fire and within days a layman successfully moved a motion in a meeting that Father Hawkins approach the local Catholic bishop to seek the en masse conversion of St Mary's parishioners and then that Father convey the parish's intentions to Episcopalian Church Bishop Clarence Pope.

There was a paper ballot of parishioners before Father made the approach to the Catholic bishop. It confirmed that the parishioners overwhelmingly wanted to become Catholics. Father Hawkins told listeners the Catholic bishop was understanding and supportive whereas his Episcopal counterpart was predictably disappointed, to say the least. "He told me: 'You're leaving me on the back of a sinking ship'," Father said.

Bishop Pope, one of Father's friends, was to decide in the future that he would also join the Catholic Church.

By mid-1991, the parishioners had painted over the word Episcopal in their St Mary's sign. But for a considerable time Father Hawkins and his parishioners were neither Episcopalians nor Catholics. On June 12, 1994, in what Father described as one of the most moving times of his life, his parishioners were welcomed into the Catholic Church by Bishop Joseph Delaney. Ten days later, Father Hawkins was made deacon, which he had been required to qualify for, and Bishop Delaney ordained him to the Catholic priesthood on June 29. St Mary's property came under the jurisdiction of the local Catholic diocese about the same time.

Father Hawkins said the Episcopal Church did not get in the way of the property transfer. His friend the Bishop had assured him that there would not be any obstacles facing the parish over property. Father said the Episcopal Church's hierarchy would have had to take on liabilities from a church which had just been built if they had pushed and succeeded in keeping control of St Mary's property.

Asked about changes in worshipping, Father Hawkins told the radio network that the Pope's pastoral provision allowed the congregation to retain important parts of the way it worshipped before the conversion. There was not a lot of difference between the way he and the parishioners worshipped as Catholics and what they had done as Anglicans.

Father Hawkins said that since the conversion the number of people who worshipped regularly on Sunday at St Mary's had grown significantly.

"We found ourselves to be a doorway into the Catholic Church for many people," he said.

"People are always coming to me for instructions - not only from the Episcopalian tradition but also from the Methodist faith, Baptists and so on."

The bishops of England and Wales issued a statement on April 15, 1994, to address the issue of receiving Anglicans into the Catholic Church. They said there should be no doubt that people approaching them were not simply wanting to avoid the advent of women priests.

"To describe them in such terms is inaccurate and a real disservice," the bishops said. "Rather, they reveal a depth of Catholic faith which is both impressive and moving. The doctrines they hold concerning the sacraments and the Eucharist, in particular, including its reservation for prayer and devotion, are substantially Catholic."

The bishops said it was important for the Catholic community to understand that for some Anglicans, especially clergy, the principal aim in their church life had been to help bring about the visible unity of the Church of England with the see of Peter.

In their judgment, recent decisions made this no longer a realistic possibility within the Church and led them to seek that full visible unity individually or in groups.

"Many have arrived at the conviction that visible communion with the Bishop of Rome is a necessary element of Catholic life," the bishops said. They added that it was a clear teaching of the Second Vatican Council that visible elements of the Church of Christ can and do exist outside the boundaries of the Catholic

Church. The Decree on Ecumenism recognised that these elements and sacred actions included "the celebration of the memorial of the Lord's Supper" (No.22). The bishops said this was clearly to be found in the Church of England.

Catholic teaching was that sacred actions by these Anglicans "can truly engender a life of grace and, one must say, can aptly give access to the communion of salvation" (No. 3). Based on this, the bishops said no one who was considering full communion with the Catholic Church was expected to deny the value of the liturgical life celebrated in the Church of England. In welcoming clergy approaching them, the bishops said they recognised former Anglicans priests had already exercised a call from God.

"This is the basis of our readiness to assume a continuity of ministry, normally leading to ordination to the priesthood in the Catholic Church, depending on the process of mutual discernment," they said. In all of these matters, the bishops asked for five principles to be kept in mind.

- The conviction that the fullness of Catholic life, and the orders which are part of it, is to be found in the visible communion of the Catholic Church.
- The aim for those whom seek to enter into full communion with the Catholic Church must be their eventual total integration into the life of the Catholic community.
- That those seeking full communion are required to accept the teaching authority of the Church in matters of faith and morals as exercised by the Pope, as the successor of Peter, and by the college of bishops acting in union with him.
- That there be continuing commitment to developing ecumenical relations with the Church of England and with other Churches and communities.
- The Catholic community stands to be enriched by the spiritual heritage of those seeking full communion and it is anticipated that Catholics will show generosity of heart towards new members of the community.

I'm sure that I'll always have a restful mind because changes such as women priests were not part of my agenda. I'm also sure Fathers Beyer and Williams joined me on that day in 1969 for a similar reason to mine. Our decision based on faith alone will hold us in good stead.

I knew in my heart that I was making the move based on a calling from God. It didn't matter that I almost certainly would never get to be a bishop, as the Anglican hierarchy had planned. I was content to serve God as a Catholic priest for the rest of my life.

Anglican Archbishop Appleton had wanted me to be bishop of Kalgoorlie but, being a gracious man, accepted my decision to join the Catholics. He had observed my pastoral efforts at Mt Barker and thought I was leadership material.

But some Anglican bishops and priests frowned upon my switch of allegiance. Sometime after I was ordained I had a chance meeting in Hay Street, Perth, with an Anglican priest who I thought I knew well. I greeted him with the pleasantries of the day and he responded cordially - that is until he remembered that I had joined the Catholic Church, at which time he hastily departed.

Like just about everything in the Anglican Church, there was much division over the three men who left to become Catholics. Some Anglican clergy disapproved, some were indifferent and others would have done the same thing but did not have the intestinal fortitude.

News of the Catholic Church's latest recruits led to a unique friendship with Anglican North-West Bishop Howell Witt. When Bishop Witt read in a newspaper that my children brought forward the Offertory gifts, he wrote a letter to the paper to point out that they could have taken part in a similar offering in the Anglican Church.

The Bishop and I met soon afterwards and quickly became close friends. We shared many things in common and our religious differences never became an issue - they were never discussed so arguments never arose.

Bishop Witt's wife had died and his children were adults. Little did I know that I would suffer a great loss in my life at a future time and my Anglican friend would be at the front-line giving unreservedly of his strength to help me.

Early Parishes

Scarborough

My Scarborough parishioners welcomed my family and me which was a relief because they had been asked to embrace a major change. When reporters sought their opinions on having a married priest in their parish some replied that it was a good move because it encouraged a tolerant attitude towards married priests. They said they could see advantages because a married priest would be more familiar with family problems and, therefore, better equipped to offer advice.

I didn't follow that line of thinking but didn't want to make my opinion public knowledge at the time because I didn't want to upset them. I think the celibate system serves both priests and their parishioners very well. Unmarried priests are capable of preaching on marriage as they do about the crucifixion. They've never been crucified.

Celibacy plays a pivotal role in keeping priests focused on their parishioners' needs. A priest is a member of every family and if he has a wife and children it can prevent universality. A priest should be free to visit families when they need him. A priest is Father of the flock and, as such, must not be restricted by personal family commitments.

I was blessed with a happy marriage but some clergy in the Anglican and other churches have separated and divorced after broken relationships. Such events are hardly edifying. Priests without partners can, of course, get lonely but this is a small price to pay for doing God's work - a light cross to carry especially when the joy from helping people walk on the road to eternal life is considered.

I loved Mary and our children and thanked God for them. But as switched on to life's ups and downs as Mary was, I was not permitted under Church rules to reveal my parishioners' troubles and concerns to her.

Mary was a quiet worshipper, she did not get involved in parish committees, but she was passionately opposed to abortion and made her views known to St Anne's patients. She had continued to work because my pay as a new Catholic priest was barely enough to support our family. Mary counselled against abortion and tried to persuade the Catholic hospital's patients not to have hysterectomies. She was utterly horrified by abortions, which had long been illegally done.

I worked quite happily at Scarborough for four years, though I felt the parish's senior priest was uncomfortable about having a married priest as his assistant. "How would you know, you've been ordained a month?" was one of many rhetorical questions which I learnt to tolerate. He didn't appreciate that I had been an Anglican priest for twenty five years. I think he tried to come to terms with his assistant being married but I'm certain he didn't understand me. His abruptness was just something I took in my stride, which wasn't as hard to do as one might imagine because I knew that at heart he was a good man.

Mary and the children also settled in Scarborough and I was delighted that my wife's health was much better than it had been in England. Our lifestyle was more relaxed than it ever had been and we soaked up every moment that we could, especially after living in tumultuous South Africa.

It was a time for new friendships and, although I realised that I ran the risk of compromising myself if I got too close to individual parishioners, one couple became a special part of our life. (If a priest forms a noticeably strong bond with some parishioners, other members of his congregation can feel neglected, like second-raters).

Scarborough stalwarts John and Mary Featherstone invited

my family into their home and hearts. The couple's four children and our three shared much in common and formed a formidable combination.

John said he saw me as a courageous man because I followed a tough road to Catholicism after being an Anglican priest for so many years. He helped as an acolyte when he wasn't earning a living by selling stationery. His wife was a capable schoolteacher.

Mary and I could not help but get close to the Featherstone family, whose love and support was limitless.

My work as a Catholic priest was similar in many respects to the tasks I had in the Anglican Church. I administered sacraments and had a variety of pastoral care duties. When people asked me why I converted to Catholicism, I explained that I wanted to be in communion with the Holy Father. They said they understood.

The average worshipper demonstrated much more faith than the average worshipper of today. People attended Mass and sacraments, such as Confession, regularly and their general commitment to the faith was evident. I believe that governments are at least partly to blame for the fact that there is more temptation in today's world to stray from the straight and narrow.

The right to abortion puts man's selfishness ahead of God's will for life. The murder of the innocent undermines family life.

Homosexuality is not only tolerated but seen as a right - so much so that advocates believe there would be nothing abnormal about gay couples lining up for made-to-order test tube babies.

The world's oldest profession is also on show as prostitutes strut their stuff via the mass media.

We are all too familiar with the rampant growth of the drug trade which is costing thousands more deaths every year.

The devil has influenced people, including many of our leaders, to evil and convinced them that there is no sin.

Western society, in particular, seems to have lost God's plot. Unfortunately, even the most devout Christians find it difficult to talk about sin. Talking about it is often the best step towards correcting what is wrong.

Mary and I were grateful to the Church that our girls were able to attend Mercedes College and David was able to study at Trinity College at no charge. It was a godsend because our finances were stretched, particularly when Mary decided to resign from her hospital job to spend more time with the family.

However, even in the Catholic schools of high repute the children had to carry a cross because I was a married priest. They copped plenty of ridicule because other children thought it strange that their father was also a Church Father. Married priests were unheard of - it was difficult to grasp how a dad could also be a priest.

"What does your dad do - he's a Catholic priest," was forever thrust in my children's face in the schoolyard.

I think the friendship my children enjoyed with the Featherstone four helped them to adjust to my new station in life. Even though they went to different schools and, therefore, our children had to deal with schoolyard problems on their own, the Featherstone four must have been a source of strength.

My family's change of Church direction from Anglican to Catholic was done without input from my children, which was a mistake. Mary and I had left our children out of something important for probably the first time. We had taken it for granted that they would settle, which eventually they did, but we should have handled things differently.

I think parents need to be careful about making family decisions without consulting their children, even when the children are of primary school age. Our children could have become bitter because their lives were drastically changed without explanation.

I would not say that I achieved anything out of the ordinary at Scarborough but it was reassuring when parishioners told me that they liked my style of preaching and the way I celebrated

Mass. I had a comfortable start in the Catholic Church and was far from prepared for my next assignment - the tough task of parish priest of Armadale.

Armadale

My new parishioners saw me as a stuffed shirt Englishman and were agitated because they had been landed with a married priest. I think Archbishop Goody made a mistake when he did not insist that a bishop induct me into the parish of mostly true-blue West Australians. The predominantly working-class families of the parish might have taken a different approach and treated me differently if a bishop had been seen to embrace my new challenge - the bishop could have broken the ice. I'm sure Archbishop Goody had no idea that he was sending me to a Hell on Earth.

David missed the drama. He was a boarder at the agricultural college in Narrogin. The girls were also sheltered to some extent because they continued as students of Mercedes and did not join a local school.

The children did not meet many Armadale people in the 12 months I was its parish priest. Even if they had been seen more in the community, I'm sure the locals would still not have made them welcome.

Mary and I had our faith tested many times in the Bahamas and South Africa but we had always been able to get on top of problems. But the Armadale challenge was out of left field. I was at a loss when parishioners would not accept me and made their feelings clear.

I altered the presbytery to accommodate a family which cost the parish money and made Mary and me even more unpopular. The diehards loved the old house and it could have been left as it was if a single priest had been assigned to the parish.

I bore the brunt of the criticism because I was the priest but Mary copped some offhand treatment and felt uneasy living in the parish. Despite the tension between the parishioners and us, they continued to attend Mass. In fact, young people started going back to church when I held a rock music Mass and formed the Nineteen Twelvers group for youth. Armadale parish was established in 1912, hence the Nineteen Twelvers name.

But no matter how hard I tried my heart was not in the parish - it was not the place for me and my family.

One day Mary and I went for a drive in the country and ended up visiting the sisters at Toodyay. A Sister Luke took us on a tour of their premises and showed us the presbytery. There was no priest at the parish.

"You'll live here one day," she joked. "I think this would be the very place for you."

Mary and I laughed. Little did we know that soon afterwards, when I talked the Archbishop into transferring me, we would be doing just that. I suggested to the Archbishop that Father Beyer, who was at Attadale, would be a suitable replacement for me at Armadale. I thought that some of my parishioners were mellowing on the issue of married priests and knew that being Australian, not a Brit, would go a long way towards him being accepted. Archbishop Goody thought my reasoning was sound and gave Father the challenge. He turned out to be a wise choice for the parish.

Toodyay

Jane and Mary were to be Mercedes boarders when their mother and I moved to Toodyay. Mary and I decided it was better for them to be boarders than to change schools so their education would not be disrupted. We thought it possible that I could be posted to another parish before they finished their schooling. The girls did not want to be boarders but I'm sure they realised we loved them dearly and would never have tried to offload them. Jane met a young man, Hannes Gebauer, through a mutual friend while at Mercedes. They fell in love and were destined in later years to make a lifelong commitment to each other.

Mary and I took no time to settle in Toodyay. It was like Heaven on Earth after Armadale, though when I had announced my transfer some parishioners said they were sorry to see us leave. Some Armadale people had grown to tolerate me, maybe even like me. Maybe my work setting up the Nineteen Twelvers had turned the tide. I did not know what was behind the apparent change of heart, not that it mattered because I would not have given up the chance to shift to Toodyay.

The Toodyay presbytery was a big house in good condition. My wife and I knew we would miss our children and that they would miss us so it was comforting to know that when they came home at weekends and during holidays the family members could enjoy each other's company in a fine home.

The girls were doing well at Mercedes both academically and in terms of their personal development.

Jane was interested in the travel business, in which she was destined to work after finishing school.

Mary was gifted in financial matters and eventually would forge a career in stocks and shares.

David, who studied at Muresk Agricultural College near Northam when Mary and I shifted to Toodyay, had his sights set on the land. He was to work as a farmhand after finishing his studies and later to take up a position with the Agriculture Department.

My Toodyay role included caring for the town's residents and people in its immediate surrounds and visiting nearby farming areas to say Mass on Sunday. It was a smooth parish to steer because it was small - about 80 people in total attended the two Sunday Masses in Toodyay - and the people, many of them farmers, were amiable and keen to help me.

My arrival at the parish in 1971 was made all the smoother because parishioners had feared they would be left without a priest. When my predecessor was transferred to Perth, there had been talk that he might not be replaced. The talk was scotched by my arrival and the fact that I was married with three children never became an issue.

Mary went to work at the Northam hospital, which she said was fulfilling, and she enjoyed the company of the Toodyay parish's nuns. She had struck up a friendship with the nuns almost immediately after we arrived in town. The love the nuns had for her didn't surprise me because she was understanding, compassionate and easy to talk with. For me and through my eyes, she was the perfect wife.

I also built a strong relationship with the sisters, but it was put to a test when some of them opted out of their habit and into clothes worn by women in mainstream society. The nuns' superior came to me one day and asked that I bless a rosary. "Go away and don't come back until you're dressed properly," I growled.

Our relationship was on shaky ground for some time, until I

Father Lisle marries a young couple at St John the Baptist Church, Toodyay

realised the nuns' decision to dress in lay clothes was part of a much wider movement and I would have to come to terms with it. A few orders were to stay in their full habits but many others were to relax their dress rules. I would never embrace such changes in dress standards.

In my opinion, relaxing the rules has been one of many changes in convents which has seen them become worldly and, in some cases, not unlike women's clubs. Some nuns now have the latest hair perms, drive fast cars and behave like women outside convents. There are some people who think this helps nuns to communicate with Mr and Mrs Average Citizen and their children, but I feel they risk losing respect. A nun's habit bears witness to her faith - it makes a statement. The habit also helps people to find nuns in times of need.

Toodyay's Mercy Sisters ran a motor mission which involved them travelling to schools in the district to teach catechism, Church doctrine. I thought they should be more visible as nuns in the community they served so well.

Of course, I had always held a similar opinion about the priestly collar. It made a statement and I knew non-Catholics as well as Catholics respected me because I wore my collar. I believed that priests who tried to be one of the people by wearing mainstream clothes and putting aside their collars were going down the wrong track.

Priests aren't Mr Averages in many ways nor does the laity consider them as such or want them to act as such. A priest's collar bears witness to what he believes in and shows he is proud to be doing God's work. It goes without saying that a priest's collar puts him in the public eye and brings responsibilities.

Catholic priests throughout the Ages have been held in high esteem by their parishioners. In fact, they've been put on a pedestal and, in many cases, the people have followed what Father has said without questioning it.

It was evident when my children visited that the Toodyay

nuns related well with young people. I was delighted that David and the girls felt comfortable being around them because I was tied to the parish, especially at the weekend, and got very few opportunities for family outings. I was unlike most fathers, who could take a break on Sunday to go on a picnic or some other family get-together.

My children were raised knowing their father loved them very much but also aware of the restrictions I faced at the weekend.

The children were brought up with plenty of discipline because all the members of our family led disciplined lives. Thank God, all three kids were well adjusted and by the time Mary and I moved to Toodyay had become quite independent.

Most of the Toodyay parishioners loved life and their happy disposition gave me a lot of joy as their priest.

My busy Sunday started with Mass at Toodyay, followed by trips to nearby districts such as Wundowie, Bakers Hill and Jennacubbine. There were only a handful of people in the communities outside of Toodyay who joined me for Mass but I could tell by their looks that they were pleased when I arrived so I was more than happy to serve them.

Sunday was a demanding day but one almost all priests expect to be busy and, hopefully, the day in the week we most look forward to.

My Monday to Saturday duties did little to stretch me, especially compared with some of the challenges I came across as a young Anglican priest.

As part of my pastoral care work, I regularly visited my Toodyay parishioners after Mass on weekdays. I drew up a roster hoping and praying not to leave anyone off it. There were times when people would knock on my door seeking help, but these were few and far between. And the worries of most people who came to me never seemed insurmountable - Toodyay was that kind of place.

I had many quiet times and when there were parish activities to organise, I was never short of volunteers to help me carry the load. The spare time presented an opportunity to hone my writing ability.

The Northam Advertiser newspaper offered me a column which I was delighted to accept because it gave me another avenue to reach people. I had had a column in an Armadale paper and knew the media, which annoyed us so much after my ordination, also could be used to spread God's word.

As is generally par for the course for Catholic priests, I was left to get on with running the parish with minimal interference from the Church hierarchy. There were visits by the bishop and I was required to attend clergy meetings but by and large I was my own boss.

One of the biggest annual events in the parish was a Latin Mass, at which the Diocesan Choir sang, followed by a family picnic. The mystery of the Latin Mass was made all the more attractive by the choir's performance. St John the Baptist Church was always packed to the rafters with people, many of whom had travelled hundreds of kilometres to listen to the Perth-based singers.

One year when the choir performed, a couple who had just shifted to the district came to their first Mass in Toodyay. They had no idea it was a special event. When they heard beautiful Latin singing, something they had never experienced, in the small town's church they were pleasantly shocked. They told me being in the church was like Heaven on Earth. They were most disappointed when they realised it was a yearly event and that the choir would not be returning the next Sunday.

Trials and Triumphs

Penang

But not everything sailed along smoothly for Mary and I during our seven years in Toodyay.

A few years into our stay, Mary was confronted with what I'm sure would have to be one of the biggest hurdles to confront any woman. She discovered a lump in a breast which her doctor diagnosed as cancer. The mastectomy was done at St John of God Hospital at Subiaco.

It was impossible for me as a man to understand the emotional turmoil she faced. All I could do was to reassure her of my love for her and listen if she wanted to talk. To add to the burden, I had a recurrence of the prostate problems I suffered in South Africa and my specialist decided the prostate gland would have to go.

I thought Mary and I needed a holiday so after the operations I booked at a travel agency for us to get away to Singapore and Malaysia. We stayed a couple of nights in Singapore and then went to Kuala Lumpur before catching a plane to Penang.

When we arrived in Penang, I asked a receptionist at our hotel how to contact the local archbishop because I wanted to say Mass. She told me that he was out of the city and that the vicar-general was running the diocese. I thanked her for Monsignor Aloysius' phone number, walked to our room and rang him. I don't know what he thought when I replied "we will" to his invitation to meet him but the silence which followed my words of acceptance indicated to me that he was surprised.

A group of students at the Penang seminary

Mary and John Lisle living it up in Malaysia with a local

It was clear when I introduced Mary to him the next day that had he learnt over the phone about my marriage, he would have been utterly shocked.

He looked us up and down. "Are you sure that you're allowed to say Mass," he asked. "Yes, of course, I'm a priest," I replied.

It then dawned on him that he had read stories about me in newspapers and that I was the genuine article.

"Oh, you're a convert," he exclaimed. "Yes, yes, I've read all about you in the papers."

He was an elderly Indian of short stature with a big stomach. As he got excited his little tongue popped out of his mouth and his tummy went up and down, up and down. Mary and I found it too much of a challenge to hold back laughter. We didn't want to be impolite but we thought his bodily movements were hysterical.

As it turned out, there was no need to try to hide our laughter because Monsignor Aloysius had a wonderful sense of humour. As I would get to know over coming years, it was one of his many qualities which made him an easy person to love and fun to be around. No one would have blamed him for being suspicious of Mary and I at that first meeting. After all, married priests were unheard of.

Father was about to have a meal with a group of priests from the local seminary and asked us to join them. We accepted and he left us for a short time while he went ahead into the dining room, mainly to warn them. While we waited for him to return, we overheard him ask his friends: "Would you like to meet a priest from Australia with his missus?"

Father Soter Fernandez, the head of the seminary, who years later was made Archbishop of Kuala Lumpur, was among the priests we met during dinner. He invited us to look over the seminary and we accepted. But when we visited the seminary the following day, we couldn't help but notice how we were politely kept away from talking to the students. I suppose he didn't want them to learn that I was married because it would have been difficult to explain it to them.

But the wider community was to learn of my union with Mary and about our children within a few weeks. After arrangements were made for me to say Mass, a number of Penang people heard about my wife and word got around in no time. The locals seemed surprised but they did not seem to mind that I was married and two fathers rolled into one.

Mary and I had a memorable holiday and made some lifelong friends. Monsignor Aloysius asked if I would return annually so I offered to spend at least a few weeks a year helping him at his parish.

Back home in Toodyay, we got on with life - the time we spent on holiday had helped Mary to come to terms with the loss of her right breast.

Northam

I knew that Archbishop Goody had confidence in me so when he presented me with the opportunity to be Dean of Northam, I grabbed it with both hands. There had been a lot of good times during the seven years we lived in Toodyay but I needed another adventure.

My new role meant I had a number of responsibilities similar to those entrusted to a bishop. I relished the challenges because I was never likely to be promoted to bishop - the Catholic hierarchy had taken one of its biggest steps in years when it accepted me as a married priest. So being Dean of Northam was a feather in my cap and I was determined to show the Archbishop that my appointment had been a wise choice.

The Archbishop relied on me to guide the young priests in my area. I suppose having a 60-year-old priest with wide experience made him feel comfortable that local parishes would be run properly. If any of the priests were kicking over the traces, I would deal with them and report to the Archbishop.

I had a curate, Father Joe Walsh, to help me in Northam and I also was responsible for overseeing the parishes of Toodyay, York, Wongan Hills, Goomalling, New Norcia and Moora. Local brothers and nuns called on me for advice and support. I did not have authority in their line of service but they were aware of my rapport with the Archbishop and knew a few words to him on their behalf could go a long way.

My life in Northam compared with Toodyay was like chalk and cheese. There was never a dull moment in Northam. There was always something going on in the town and I was involved in much of it.

The Northam church, bigger than some churches in the metropolitan area, was often packed on Sunday. It held about 300 people at a squeeze. I also had chaplaincy duties at the big local school, St Joseph's, run by the Marist Brothers.

Mary Lisle, left, with fellow nurses at Northam hospital

When Father Walsh was transferred to a Perth parish, I was joined by the able and willing Father Thomas McDonald. He was a first-class curate and later a wonderful senior priest. In later years, he was to be appointed Dean of St Mary's Cathedral, Perth, and was made a Monsignor.

There wasn't a priest at Meckering so I would visit when I could, or had the courage to. Meckering was included in my Northam parish round. I was always nervous about venturing into the area - it was impossible to clear my mind of the 1968 earthquake in which homes were damaged, roads raised and farmland cracked. When I went to Meckering, I said Eucharistic Prayer Number 2, the shortest of the Eucharistic prayers. It meant that my visit could be brief. After Mass, I wasted no time getting in my car and heading for home, where I felt much safer. When all was said and done, there was no way for me to know if or when another earthquake would hit Meckering.

Mary and I were as happy in Northam as we had been in Toodyay. We lived close to the hospital, which pleased Mary because she had grown tired of driving between Toodyay and Northam to work.

Our home was one of the earliest built in Northam. It was built to be a presbytery, had been well maintained and had lots of space, which was great for our children and other visitors.

I took kindly to Northam and it to me from the first day we arrived - just as well because it was to be my home for eight years. The beauty of the town and district was hard to equal anywhere I had been in the world and the people were friendly and welcoming.

However, I was to endure failure as well as enjoy success.

One of my biggest flops concerned working alongside an Anglican priest on local projects. I wasn't any good at it from the outset because of my bias. Discussions which were aimed at building bridges between the churches invariably ended in disagreements. Being a former Anglican, I was at odds with my

Father John Lisle prepares to bless competitors before an Avon Descent.

counterpart on countless matters. My curate was a much better negotiator with the Anglicans than I was and ever likely to be.

I looked forward to the Avon Descent, one of the biggest events for the Northam district. Blessing the competitors before they started the gruelling whitewater boat race gave me great pleasure because it meant the organisers, some with apparently little faith, saw a need for the Church to be involved. The man who first approached me for the event's competitors, family and friends to be blessed had told me he was scarcely a Christian. Several thousand people gathered around the rostrum where I stood for the blessing.

As I prayed, some of the people in the crowd made the sign of the cross while others just looked on. There were a few people who did not want the blessing, but their attitude did not bother me - all priests expect to face challenges.

I also got the job of blessing any new ambulance bought for

Northam, even when the local St John Ambulance chiefs were not Catholics. It was another important community role for me.

From time to time a local issue would stir me and I would speak out in no uncertain terms, including during my Sunday sermon.

It was frustrating, to say the least, when hotel bars in Northam and Toodyay opened on Good Friday. People who would have been a lot better off going to the Stations of the Cross at church instead would look for the nearest pub.

It was illegal for the pubs to open but that did not stop most publicans. One of the publicans I spoke to about the practice of opening on Good Friday agreed that it was the wrong thing to do. But he said his hotel would stay open because it was tough trying to make ends meet and his takings on Good Friday were welcome.

I urged my parishioners to boycott his hotel and those of other publicans who did the wrong thing but I was preaching to the converted. The people who most needed to hear what I had to say about the issue were in the pubs.

There was little unoccupied time in my schedule.

When I got the opportunity to relax, I often spent the time in the local library. One day I decided to take a look in the English Catholic Directory and came across the name of my Andros companion, Gordon Bennett, who I hadn't heard from for many years. He had converted to Catholicism and was a parish priest at Portsmouth in England.

I was not overly surprised. We had lost contact with each other and no one had told me that Gordon had given up being an Anglican but I knew that, like me, he had a leaning towards the Catholic faith when we were young men on Andros.

Several months after finding Gordon's name in the directory, I decided to phone him. I did not know why I was making the call other than it felt like the right thing to do. We spoke briefly about each other's different Christian journey and I told him that

Northam had much to offer. "If you want to settle in WA, I will speak to Archbishop Foley on your behalf," I said. (Archbishop Goody had retired and had been replaced by Joseph Foley).

Gordon said he would think it over.

Some time later, he phoned me to say that he would like to move to WA. I spoke to Archbishop Foley and he arranged for Father Bennett to be chaplain of the Little Sisters of the Poor in Glendalough, Perth.

A matter of months later, when I found myself short of a curate, Archbishop Foley rang to inform me that Gordon would be joining me in Northam. We had faced many challenges on Andros and I was looking forward to Gordon being curate and working alongside me once again.

Father Gordon Bennett converted from Anglican to Catholic.

The Death of my Beloved Mary

Life was tougher than it had ever been for me. Mary, the children and I were carrying a cross which we were only just managing to bear. We certainly would not have been able to carry it without the love and support of God.

Mary had complained about pains in one of her shoulders and in her ribs and, when I had taken her to a doctor, our worst fears were realised.

After several years in remission, cancer was spreading uncontrollably in her body. It would take my angel, and the best mother our children could have had, away from us in less than a year.

To make matters worse, we were to have no option but for her to be admitted at St John of God Hospital in Belmont. It was not practical for me to care for her at home because she was fast becoming an invalid as her body degenerated.

As everyone who has lost loved ones to a slow death knows, there are no words that really describe the emotional turmoil.

I was helpless. It made me wonder how families which lacked faith and were in similar situations to the one in which we found ourselves could possibly cope. God helped the children and me come to terms with the fact that Mary was not long for this world.

It was reassuring to us that she held firmly to her faith, but she had some particularly testing times. The night before she died she whispered to me: "I don't want to die. John, I'm afraid."

I looked at her gently, held her hands and reminded her

of a time in South Africa when she told me about seeing a vision of Our Lady in a church.

"I did see Mary," she said adamantly.

When I met the beautiful woman I was destined to marry her faith was ordinary, if not poor. I'm sure that she became an Anglo-Catholic largely because I was an Anglo-Catholic priest. She was more an Anglo-Catholic in name than by conviction. But she attended Mass and prayed with me.

In Humansdorp, we had a routine of going to a church together every night to pray. Mary would pray in the church at night even when I was away from home on church business.

I was never likely to forget my return home after one particular Synod meeting. Mary was noticeably different in herself than before I left for the meeting but I couldn't put my finger on a reason for the change. She was at peace with everything and had absolute trust in God.

She asked me to make arrangements for her to attend Confession in Port Elizabeth. Where she wanted to go to Confession did not surprise me because we knew that I would not be hearing her Confession. Priests don't hear the Confessions of loved ones for obvious reasons. But I was taken aback that she wanted to go to Confession at all because she had been against going at any time anywhere.

While we were making our way home from Port Elizabeth, after she had made her Confession, I told her that I thought she had changed and asked for a reason. She explained that when I was at the Synod meeting, she had seen a vision of Our Lady in the Humansdorp church's chancel.

I'm not sure whether my Mary knew how to describe her experience or whether she decided to leave it in her private thoughts, but she never went into it in detail. However, it was obvious she believed she had seen a vision of Jesus' mother in the chancel.

It was clear to me that the vision was behind the change in

my wife's life but I left it at that, not wanting to intrude by questioning her in order to satisfy my curiosity. After the event, she wanted to become a Catholic but chose to wait until we were both ready to make the move.

The angel who God had blessed me with, a mother her children would always be proud of, died about 3.50pm on December 4, 1985. She was 60.

I had no doubt that she got a front-row seat in Heaven.

Two bishops and forty priests concelebrated at the funeral in St Mary's Cathedral in the heart of Perth and later my angel's human shell was laid to rest at Karrakatta.

The gift of faith helped the children and me adjust to being without Mary. Catholic Church clergy, my parishioners and other friends, including some Anglicans, provided a source of endless support.

Mary had touched the lives of many people from many walks of life. Everybody who had known her seemed to have formed a rapport with her. I was told by a number of women who had formed friendships with Mary that her commitment to her faith had helped them on their Christian journeys.

It was especially difficult facing the first Christmas without Mary, but the children and I knew that life had to go on and the comfort we gave to each other brought us closer.

We had special private memories about Mary as well as fond family ones. My daughter, Mary, must have treasured her mother being able to attend her wedding. She married Perth upholsterer Tony Di Lucia on November 9 - just 25 days before her mother died.

I knew my wife would struggle to get to the wedding but being there was precious to both mother and daughter and Mary managed to attend in a wheelchair.

Euthanasia was not a legal option but, if it had been, my family still would have agreed with me that it was not what God planned for His children, even for somebody in terrible pain.

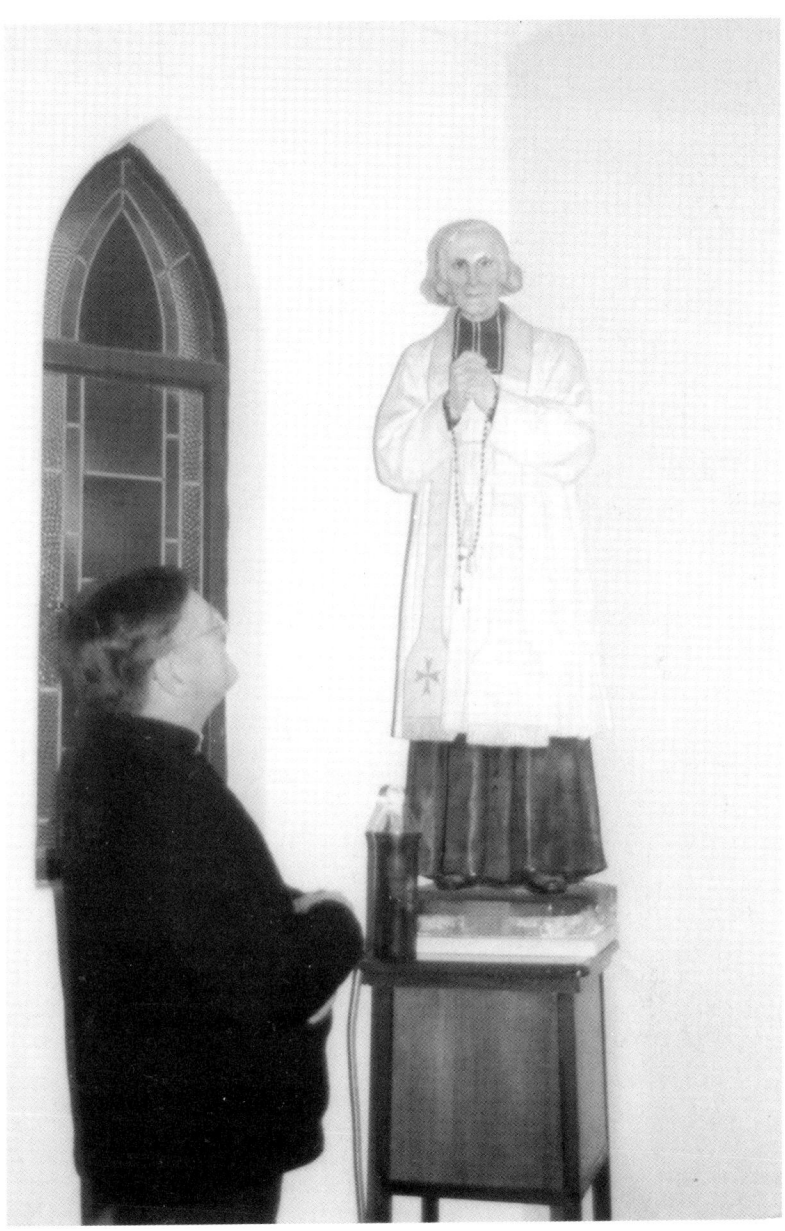

Father Lisle stays firm to his faith after the loss of his wife, Mary. He looks at a statue of the patron saint of parish priests, John Vianney, in the Northam church.

Decisions about life and death should be left to God - no one has the right to end life. This is an integral part of the Catholic faith, and I thanked God that Mary and our children held steadfastly to it.

Mary received Holy Communion daily in hospital and I was sure God was giving her the grace to handle her ordeal. I believed then and after Mary's death that if a dying person puts their trust in God, then the person's demeanour will be such that he or she will cope with their pain.

The power of prayer is limitless, but sadly it is often underestimated by people in difficult circumstances. Of course, prayer does not guarantee recovery, but it does bring sick people close to God and helps them to endure what they face. I recommend Mary Malone's Prayer for Healing:

Heavenly Father, I call on You right now in a special way.
It is through Your power that I was created.
Every breath I take, every morning I wake and every moment of every hour I live under Your power.
Father, I ask You now to touch me with that same power.
For if You created me from nothing, You can certainly recreate me.
Fill me with the healing power of Your spirit.
Cast out anything that should not be in me.
Mend what is broken.
Root out any damaged cells.
Open any blocked arteries or veins and rebuild any damaged areas.
Remove all inflammation and cleanse any infection.
Let the warmth of Your healing love pass through my body to make new any unhealthy areas so that my body will function the way You created it to function.
And, Father, restore me to full health in mind and body so that I may serve You the rest of my life.
I ask this through Christ our Lord. Amen.

On the day that Mary died, I recorded her death in my personal diary. It was a straight-out entry. Next day, I wrote more in the diary. I wrote: "My darling went to her rest yesterday and life will never be the same again."

A year after Mary died, I wrote in the same diary: "My darling's first anniversary today - God love her."

The Christian understanding of death helped the children and me to stay focused on rebuilding our lives.

When God created the world He made it good and without death. He then tested Adam and Eve, who had free will, for loyalty and obedience. They were not to eat the fruit from a tree in a garden. But Satan tempted Eve to disobey God, telling her that eating from the tree would provide knowledge of good and evil, and that she would be like a god. Eve ate from the tree and tempted Adam to do likewise. After they had eaten, they became naked and hid from God. But eventually they had to face their creator. When God asked Adam if the couple had disobeyed Him, Adam admitted committing the sin. God then turned the pair out of the garden and made Satan go on his belly.

The story puts forward the premise that God gave the first people in the world a test - the story need not be taken verbatim.

Man has free will to accept or reject God, to love Him or hate Him. No one is forced to love God, no one is forced to hate God. The calamities in the world, which started the day Adam and Eve disobeyed God, are due to people misusing free will. Rejecting God has given Satan the power to bring disease and sickness into the world.

Disasters are the result of man's own doing - of sin. But God is the source of grace when a person is dying and offers eternal life. God alone has the right to end life as He has to start it, and God has offered eternal life to those people who follow Him. Christians believe God will call them to His home when He is ready. The children and I obviously wanted Mary to recover from cancer - her ordeal was devastating and we loved her dearly.

But we accepted that God called her and we knew He helped her while she was dying.

There have been many natural and man-made disasters in the world over the course of time and, no doubt, many more are yet to come. These disasters have taken thousands and thousands of lives and brought much sadness to loved ones left behind. But sometimes people have been brought together and sometimes afflictions have pushed people to learn from mistakes.

In January, 2001, in the worst natural disaster to befall India in modern times, an earthquake which measured 7.9 on the Richter scale killed thousands of people in Gujarat State and left thousands of others injured and homeless. Chief Minister Keshubhai Patel said the death toll could reach 22,000. Unofficial estimates put the death toll at 50,000.

Poverty and corruption which makes cutting corners on building projects a routine practice puts the poor most at risk in earthquake-prone India so it is not surprising that these people were hit hard. But out of the ruins some good emerged.

Pakistan, India's long-time foe over the Kashmir region, was quick to join other countries around the world in offering aid. The tragedy brought much heartbreak, but it also prompted more fortunate people to be benevolent.

After learning about the tragedy, I couldn't help but think how much better off the people who were killed would be in Heaven than those people who barely survive in the country's poverty. They would experience joy rather than sorrow, probably for the first time.

In August 1999, more than 12,000 people were killed in an earthquake in Turkey that measured 7.4 on the Richter scale. Turkey's Prime Minister, Bulent Ecevit, reportedly said past governments bore some responsibility for shoddy construction that contributed to the high death toll. He said people had a right to be angry. The mistakes of the past that cost so many lives should not be repeated in the future.

When the Russian submarine, Kursk, sank to the bottom of the Barents Sea in August 2000, some of the country's former foes, such as Britain, offered to help in the rescue. The world saw what appeared to be a race to rescue any survivors in the submarine, which was 110m below the sea's surface.

Russia fell to the sin of pride when it initially refused the offers of help.

Later, officials said that all one hundred and eighteen men aboard the Kursk had died when the submarine was flooded after a massive explosion during naval exercises. Whether any sailors survived the explosion or not, whether any sailors were alive as oxygen began to run out in the submarine is not the issue. Countries once enemies of Russia acted in good faith and Russia had the opportunity to accept help.

My life moved on without Mary - it had to. God had wanted her to be with Him and there were a number of people He had left me to care for as a priest. In some of my few quiet times in the Northam parish I reflected on my happy marriage. I knew one of the most important ingredients in any strong, happy relationship was selfless love.

If a husband and wife give to one another in unselfishness, never putting personal desires ahead of their partner's, the marriage has a good opportunity to succeed.

In my opinion, a husband and wife should take different roles. I believe the husband should be the dominant factor and that he is, even in most marriages in our modern Western world. But a man must not be domineering towards his wife.

Saint Paul told husbands to love their wives as they, the husbands, loved themselves.

The woman, in my view, should take a passive line to a certain degree. She has a duty to follow her husband within reasonable circumstances, such as if he believes it is best for the family to relocate from one city to another for employment.

When Christians get married before an altar, they face a

crucifix. Pagans find it impossible to understand that the crucifix stands for unselfish love. Jesus' death on the cross set the highest example of unselfishness. His example is the one all husbands and wives must attempt to follow.

Sadly, many people entering marriage do not understand, or want to understand, the unselfish message in Jesus' death on the cross. Separation and divorce have become easy options in the Western world.

True Friends

I was blessed as much by the different sorts of people who were my friends as by the many friends I had. The young people in my life kept me up-to-date with the changing trends they faced in the community - some which presented them as Christians with tough tests.

Peter Jack was among the closest of my young friends. I had met Peter, from Perth, before Mary died. The young accountant landed a job in Northam and planned to stay at a hostel until he found somewhere better to live. But when he arrived in town, on Easter Tuesday, the hostel was closed.

Despite the muddle he was in, Peter found time to go to evening Mass. He met a local nun after Mass who steered him in my direction. When he told me that the hostel was shut, I offered him a bed for the night.

Next day Mary said to me: "What are you going to do about Peter? I think he should stay with us, we've got plenty of room and he could stay if he was our David."

The thought was typical of what I had come to expect from Mary. She was always thoughtful of others - never shy to take in a stranger.

I put the offer to Peter, who was very appreciative and accepted.

It was the start of strong bond between the three of us - Peter fitted in with Mary and me like an adopted son. He lived with us for five years before he moved back to the city.

Peter was a devout Catholic so it did not surprise me when he pursued his career through Church organisations. His career

Peter Jack, front row right, prepares to sit an acolyte exam with fellow parishioners

blossomed and in later years he was appointed chief executive of Southern Cross Homes WA, which provided residential care for elderly people. He then went on to be finance and administration manager for Mercy Community Services, which offered a wide range of care services.

A young man I met in Northam after Peter left town never got the chance to meet Mary which was a shame because they also would have become close. And little did I know when I met him but local newspaper journalist John Logan would one day be helping me to tell my life story in this book.

John, in his mid 20s, looked sharp enough when we met at the newspaper when I was submitting my weekly column. But, for whatever reason, I suspected that he was lost about life.

"You've just arrived in town, so where are you living? Have you found somewhere yet?" I asked him.

"Who knows Father because I don't," John replied. "I've

got a flat in Scarborough but I can't travel back there every night. I'll probably settle for a room in one of the pubs for at least a few nights of the week and commute between home in Perth and here during the rest of the week."

I offered him a bed in the presbytery as I had done for Peter five years earlier. I could not help but notice that John was taken aback for a moment, but he wasted no time regaining composure.

"I can't expect you to do that for me," he said politely.

I told him that there was room for him in the presbytery and that he would be made welcome. He decided to give it a go during the week and to travel home to Perth at the weekend.

We got on fabulously once he settled in to his new surrounds and he grew to trust me in a way that all true friends trust each other. He had been raised by Catholic parents, timber worker Jack Logan and wife Alice, of Manjimup. They loved him very much but, like so many young people, he also needed an outside influence to help him focus on the right path in life.

John stayed for about four months before returning to the city to build a sound career in journalism. By the time he turned 40 he had worked for The West Australian newspaper for almost ten years.

He attributed his success to his parents sticking by him through thick and thin and to guidance from myself and his grandparents at times when he could easily have gone completely off the rails.

John and I would especially remember one night during his stay in Northam.

John was woken by a big, unkempt Aboriginal man who slammed a door as he made his way inside the presbytery. The door had been left unlocked, which wasn't unusual on hot nights. Before John knew it, the man was in the bedroom, reeking of alcohol and demanding money for food.

"Got some money for me brother? I'm hungry brother and got to get money," the unwelcome visitor said.

John was not impressed but apparently didn't let on. He just quietly led the man out of the bedroom to the back porch, found him a chair and told him to wait.

"Got no money but you can have this leg of roast lamb," he told the visitor when he returned from the kitchen. "On your way now, I've got to sleep. Good luck to you."

The man left. He didn't realise the lamb which John gave him would have been put out with our rubbish the next morning - it had been deemed unfit for human consumption.

When I was told the story in the morning, I didn't know what to say. It was one of the few times in my life I had been left speechless.

I often had had late-night visitors and knew it was wise to lock the house because some people did not have genuine reasons for calling on me. There was no point giving them money because they would waste it and I would have less for people with real needs.

What John had done was un-Christian but I thought that he must have been frustrated by not being left to sleep. I also knew, and I'm sure that John was aware as well, that the man probably had a strong constitution after years of heavy drinking.

Years later, John decided to be a voluntary worker for Perth-based Aboriginal radio station 6AR. Maybe he was making amends for that hot night when he gave the much less than average meat dish to his unexpected Aboriginal visitor. He told me that he had come to admire those Aboriginal people who strive to better themselves and that he was keen to encourage and help them.

Elizabeth O'Shaughnessy was another friend who stood by me as I got on with life after Mary died. Elizabeth was in life's twilight when I met her, before Mary died, but her energy seemed endless. She was of high English stock but never let on about it. Her father was a viscount, she had been married to a viscount and she had spent a lot of her life socialising with British royalty. After her second husband died, she joined her daughter and son-in-law, Penny and Tony Motion, who ran historic Buckland Homestead near Northam.

"Father, I've heard that your wife is very ill," Elizabeth said after Mass one morning. "Is there anything I can do for you?" She hadn't met Mary.

"Can you cook?" I asked her, knowing very little about her background at the time.

"I'm cooking for my family at Buckland Homestead and when I'm finished, I'll help you," she said.

If I had been aware of her esteemed background, I would not have asked her to cook for Mary and me. Being English, I knew that making such a request wasn't the done thing. But, as it turned out, Elizabeth was far from being a snob. She told very few people about her association with royalty and often rolled up her sleeves to help people in the local community.

The Buckland Homestead property, 13km from Northam, was settled in 1836. It was a showplace of history and the Motions provided bed and breakfast accommodation. Elizabeth was in her element living in a cottage on the property.

She became close to Mary and, even though my wife was suffering from cancer, they shared many happy times. Elizabeth was always looking for ways to ease Mary's load, such as by cooking, and was a great comfort to her and me in the last months before Mary died.

After I lost Mary, Elizabeth visited me several times a week to see if I was coming to terms with my wife's death and getting on with life. She often joined me for a traditional English breakfast after early Mass during the week and was a willing, reliable helper in the parish. Her humble nature and generosity towards others set an example for people.

We shared a lot in common and our bond of friendship grew stronger. It was impossible not to get close, despite my policy of keeping parishioners at a distance to prevent any potential for jealousy.

My work in the parish was manifold, but there were some challenges that I relished more than others. My responsibility to nurture the students of St Joseph's School was one that I grabbed with both hands. I loved helping children and had seen every opportunity to be involved in teaching them about the Catholic faith as a gift from God.

St Joseph's had many teachers who were putting its girls and boys on the right path for life so my task of instructing the students about the faith was made all the easier.

I had always believed that instructing young people was one of the most important roles of a priest and it came as no surprise to many people I knew when I decided the big primary and secondary school would have a full-time chaplain. I wanted the students at the school, run by laity, to have daily contact with a priest and had become concerned because my time at the school was limited by other responsibilities.

The value of having priests, brothers or nuns around schools has been underestimated. Sadly, cases of abuse, raised in the media, have tainted the work of the majority of religious people who are dedicated to serving God through helping our youth.

Catechists also have an important role to play in preparing young people for Christian life as adults.

St Joseph's students came from a variety of backgrounds. Some were from families at the lower end of the income scale - private schooling was affordable to more people than it is today. Most students were members of Catholic families, as could be expected, but some non-Catholics had met the school's criteria and were welcome. I was pleased that non-Catholics were invited to study at the school because it gave them and their parents the chance to experience our faith and helped Catholic students and teachers to mix with people from the wider community.

I continued to give lessons at the school when I could. The lessons I gave while Dean of Northam covered a big range of issues, including sex and abortion. I could see that morals were increasingly being dismissed in the modern world and wanted the students to guard against sin and stay focused on God.

It was the 1980s and one did not have to be a Rhodes scholar to realise that sex was widely available.

The virtues of young people were being bombarded in society. The media didn't help - too much attention was paid by radio, television and newspapers to people challenging long established moral rules and views. I conceded that some changes were for the better, but many others meant fewer standards and more moral decay. Advertisements and television programs which reflected, if not promoted, promiscuity in society concerned me. It seemed sex was OK just about anywhere at anytime between a number of bodies as long as participants used contraceptives.

I reminded St Joseph's students that a breaking down of moral standards was diametrically opposed to the Church's teachings. We talked about the sacredness of the human body and I explained that the only appropriate place for sex was in marriage.

The Holy Spirit comes to live inside the body at Confirmation. The person's body becomes a temple of the Holy Spirit through the sacrament, and so he or she must act in a responsible way. Immorality is irresponsible - it takes people away from God.

I also enjoyed less serious conversations with the school's young people. Where appropriate, I would encourage them to express themselves in the parish community. I told them that the Mass was central to the faith of all Catholics, young and not so young, and it had long been my view that teenagers should be given the opportunity to help the priest and fellow parishioners to choose some of its music. However, the Mass was not to be turned into an entertainment - it was not a show. A line had to be drawn somewhere to keep the Mass set apart as the greatest communion we have with God.

The Northam parish's choir gave people of different ages and backgrounds the chance to worship God together. The Sunday

Mass at which the choir performed always drew the most parishioners. The church was often packed. A friend, Justin Bowen, was among the talented singers. The choir was well run by choir mistress Eleanor Cummins, who was also the school's secretary.

The Northam church was well attended

Life from the Back Seat

Mosman Park

As the age of 70 began to rise on life's horizon, the many tasks associated with the Northam parish and surrounding districts were starting to wear me down. I became too tired to continue as Dean of Northam so I asked Archbishop Foley for a post as a priest of a smaller parish. I realised that as I was ageing, I needed to take a back seat in the Catholic Church.

The Mosman Park parish was vacant, which I saw as a godsend because I had been interested in the position for a long time. The parish was well established and I knew that I would be able to handle the workload.

But the diversity between parishioners and how it had been handled was reason for concern.

The Corpus Christi Church's pews were arranged in such a way that there was a gap about halfway between the altar and the church entrance. Rich people almost invariably sat on the pews before the gap and, therefore, were closest to the altar. The poor sat behind them.

The Offertory gifts were put in the gap and brought before the altar by wealthy members of the congregation. Poor people rarely, if ever, got the honour of bringing forward the gifts.

I had had a gutful of apartheid in South Africa and, although the disparity was nowhere near the same scale, it disgusted me. I had seen and fought against some of the most unfair treatment of people in the world and was determined that my parishioners would be equal among themselves. At my first opportunity, I told parish council members about my concerns.

"I want an immediate end to this. This has got to stop," I said.

I was pleasantly surprised to find on entering the church soon after the council's meeting that the gap had been closed. The delegates had shifted the pews without question. To the best of my knowledge, none of the parish's wealthy folk left as a result of what had been done. To the contrary, the atmosphere at Sunday Masses seemed more relaxed and more people went to church. When Saturday night Mass at the nearby Swanbourne church ended, my church's Saturday vigil was packed.

I thought afterwards that perhaps there were no surreptitious motives behind the gap that had troubled me so much. The space had provided additional room to move at Communion and the pews had probably been arranged towards that end. But no matter why the gap had been created, it had gone forever. I was sure the change had been for the better and I was set on bringing my parishioners closer together irrespective of their different financial backgrounds.

I was delighted when parishioners told me that they felt welcome at Mass. They said fellowship at morning tea after Sunday Mass helped them to get to know one another better. An Asian lady, who I understand was rich, told me that she had been attending Mass at the church for years but no one had spoken to her before I arrived.

I was slowing down but it was the late 1980s and I was far from afraid of making changes if they were needed.

Billy Madden, who had lived in the presbytery for many years, was one of the parish's mainstays. Billy, in his late 70s, was an acolyte at the early weekday Masses and he led the rosary on several occasions. His other duties included locking the church at night about six o'clock, opening up early next morning and checking church equipment, such as microphones. Perth had more than its share of thieves and vandals which meant the church had to be locked overnight.

Billy's wife had died and he had decided to help the parish priest whenever and wherever he could. I could rely on Billy to lock up and check the church's security lights, but that did not guarantee a thieves-free zone. It did not surprise me when someone broke into the sacristy. I think it was fortunate that little was stolen and that damage was minimal.

The Mosman Park parish ran smoothly most of the time and, as I had expected, there was much less work than I had had at Northam. Unlike my former parish, I had little involvement with a school. The nearby Iona Presentation College had a capable chaplain. My involvement with Iona amounted to no more than graciously accepting invitations to school concerts and other functions.

One night, sitting quietly in the presbytery office, I decided to make some phone calls. Monsignor Aloysius wasn't on the list of people I was due to call but I always liked talking with him and ended up dialling his number.

As soon as I heard his voice, I knew he was seriously ill. He told me that he had been in bed but that he was pleased I had called him.

It was the last time I spoke to my friend - he died, aged 91, a few days after our conversation. We had been friends for more years than I could remember and shared many happy times at his St Francis Xavier parish during my annual holidays. I knew I would miss him very much and my faith-enriching trips to South-East Asia.

In fact, I missed Asia so much after a few years that I decided to write to the Archbishop of Singapore, Gregory Yong, to ask him if any priest would be interested in providing short-stay accommodation for me. I was keen to say Mass and help a local priest because I knew the fervent faith of the country's people would be uplifting.

Father Ho, who I had met several years earlier in Penang, was told about my letter at a meeting of priests and opened his presbytery's doors to me.

"I know him, I'll have him," he told the Archbishop.

Monsignor Aloysius

Father, in his 40s when I took up his offer of accommodation, was the driving force behind building the new Holy Family Church on the outskirts of Singapore city. The church, which holds about 6000 people, was often packed - such is the faith of the people of Singapore.

Of course, Sunday Masses were particularly busy for Father Ho as he was the parish's priest. He was delighted when I stayed with him because he knew I would help with the workload.

My responsibilities included saying the 6pm weekday Masses as well as some of the Sunday Masses. I also was happy to be on-call for funerals and for other times when Father wanted me to lend a hand. I was in my element preaching and sharing Mass with such big crowds committed to the faith.

Singaporeans, like the Malaysian people who grew close to my heart in earlier years, make sure Christ is a priority in their lives.

I was saddened when I thought about the malaise of many parishes in Australia and other countries in the Western world. More and more Catholics in WA were giving up going to church and proclaiming their faith. The cutting contrast left me questioning why so many Westerners had strayed and asking myself what could be done to put them back on the right track. I had few answers if any at all. Perhaps the affluence in cities like Perth led people to thinking that they did not need Christ in their lives.

In later years, Father Ho's health began to fail him and he was forced to ease up. He was transferred to a church of devotion, St Joseph's in the heart of Singapore city.

While I was at Mosman Park, I married David to Debra Chrimes, of Toodyay, and a few months later Jane to long-time boyfriend Hannes Gebauer, a dermatologist. Marrying my children was among my happiest roles since I had been ordained a Catholic priest.

I married David and Debra at St John the Baptist Church in

Toodyay on April 21, 1990. The sacredness of marriage was of utmost importance to me and I was troubled that it had become almost the norm for couples to live together before walking down the aisle. I'm not sure what my son made of it but I took the opportunity of my sermon to denounce living together and impress upon all present the importance of holy matrimony.

Jane and Hannes were married on August 18 in the Aquinas College chapel in Manning. It was familiar surrounds for Hannes - he had been an Aquinas student.

I was parish priest at Mosman Park for about six years before I decided it was time to retire.

A nun from Iona, Sister Maureen, one day told me that she thought I could have suffered a mild stroke. Perhaps I looked ash-grey to her but I felt fine and was surprised by what she had said.

But a short time later, when I was working at my office desk, I found myself in a muddle. I made an appointment with a doctor and tests confirmed what Sister Maureen had suspected.

I acknowledged that the stroke was a warning and wrote to Archbishop Barry Hickey, telling him it was time for me to retire. He had replaced Joseph Foley, who had died.

I found a unit in the Knights of the Southern Cross-run Joseph Cooke Retirement Village in Shelley before tendering my resignation to the Archbishop.

Retirement and Reflections

In 1993, at the age of 70-something, I moved in to the unit to start what I saw as the last chapter of my Christian journey.

I had no idea what retirement would be like and it worried me that I would not find enough to do. As it turned out, retirement was a poor description for my new lifestyle.

God gave me plenty of ways to contribute in the community and it was not long before my friends started to refer to me as a recycled priest.

The Servite Sisters, of Carlisle, asked me to say Mass regularly for them and to be their chaplain, which was a part-time role.

Soon afterwards, Peter Jack, who was working for Southern Cross Homes, requested that I take on Two Pines Nursing Home in Maylands. I was destined to say Mass during the week for the home's residents and help in various other ways for the next six years. Later, I would care for their spiritual needs at another home.

About a year after I started the part-time role at Two Pines, Father Michael McMahon, provincial of the Pallottine priests and brothers, phoned and said he was keen to get me involved at Murdoch University. I was in reasonably good health, especially compared with the people of Two Pines, so I agreed to the part-time chaplaincy position.

It was the right decision - the students needed support and they kept my mind alert and me feeling much younger than I was. I was in the job for five years before it got too much for me, in 2000.

I had somehow managed to juggle my commitments at the university with those at Two Pines and help the Servite Sisters as well. Two Pines was shut late in 2000 and its residents moved to Margaret Hubery House in Shelley, just a few hundred metres from my unit. The home was built by Southern Cross WA Aged Care, formerly Southern Cross Homes, and its residents include a number of elderly nuns and brothers. I was appointed chaplain when the home opened in January, 2001.

My responsibilities include saying Mass daily, making sacraments such as Confession and the Anointing of the Sick available, counselling and generally offering support. I knew when I took the job that it and helping the Servite Sisters would be as much as I could handle, with my 83rd birthday just a few months away.

Recent photograph of Father Lisle

The closest I come to parish work these days is when I'm locum for a few weeks at one of the parishes near home. I also say Mass on Sundays at Regina Coeli Church in Brentwood. My role at the home keeps me active but I get time to put my feet up for a few hours most days.

I think it is important for senior citizens who are blessed with good health to make themselves available for some sort of community work.

Over the years much has been made of young people failing to recognise the value of senior citizens, but I think that more older people should offer to help our youth. There is still no substitute for wisdom. In these days of changing technology many of the lessons of the past are still as relevant as ever. Sadly, some of our senior citizens see young people as a threat to their safety. Truth is these troublemakers are in the minority and most kids want and need help as they make their way in the world.

Experienced priests have a responsibility to nurture and encourage young priests as well as young people in the wider community. I know experienced priests have a lot to offer and I'm sure young priests and seminarians are looking for role models to help them face their many challenges. I feel blessed that many of my friends are young priests. As the old saying goes, you reap more from giving than from taking.

Sometimes the most simple advice can help.

For example, young people have a tendency to take on too much too quickly - they think and act like there is no tomorrow and risk burnout. I noticed that one young friend was rushing around to meetings and suggested that he think about the value of some of them. He took stock, made a list of priorities for himself and put his life back in order.

Of course, guidance from the top is essential for the wellbeing of any organisation, and the Catholic Church in WA is fortunate to have Archbishop Hickey. I'm sure his steady, even-handed approach has been responsible for the strength of the local Church and its well stocked seminary. The seminary often gets applications from young men abroad as well as from West Australians.

It is not easy to explain the calling a person gets to enter the religious way of life but God makes his request clear to the person He is calling. Once the call is answered positively, God gives the person direction to do His will. Faith put in God can move mountains, and it is just as well because sometimes there are a lot of mountains to move.

The challenges facing priests are many and varied. The life of unmarried priests can be lonely, especially for young priests posted to parishes in remote areas. Many priests find they're most lonely when they return to the presbytery after spending a day visiting people and have to cook the evening meal and eat alone. But the sacrifices of the life are by far outweighed by the privilege of being able to help people find and follow God. It is a life of giving to people - sometimes through sacraments, other times by offering an ear and, perhaps, some friendly advice.

A priest receives the Sacrament of Orders at his ordination to help him in his pastoral work. Saving souls is the business of the priesthood, but going about it isn't always straightforward. Sometimes people searching for God need a priest to exercise enormous patience. Sometimes people have to work through a swag of questions they have about the Church.

There are other people who just don't want to listen to the word of God. Priests must love these people as well no matter how hard it gets. However, I have found there is no point in entering into arguments with people who refuse to at least contemplate listening. If a person comes to me with a fait accompli answer, I don't enter into an argument because it is waste of time.

It saddens me that some people who have been searching have been led astray by sects which offer free and easy lifestyles but nothing concrete on which to build lives. You don't have to be a priest to realise that these sects create problems instead of helping to solve them.

As a father of three and now a grandfather of seven, I have been surrounded by young people most of my family life besides through my work as a priest. Jane is a mother of three - Xavier, 5, Portia, 7, and Christian, 9. Mary has two children - Emma, 5, and Rebecca, 10. David is a father of two - Joshua, 9, and Hannah, 10. Like most grandfathers, I look forward to seeing the children when they visit - the joy of a child and the joy the child brings is very special.

I am also moved by the way my grandchildren see me and talk about me. They are quick to tell people they meet that their grandfather is a Father in the Catholic Church and seem keen to discuss my vocation with their friends. No one else at the schools they attend has a grandad who is a priest. The interest in my life which they share with pupils and teachers helps to keep the Church a positive talking point.

Mary and Tony Di Lucia with daughters Rebecca and Emma

David Lisle with his children, Joshua and Hannah

Hannah Lisle

Joshua Lisle

Xavier, left, Portia and Christian Gebauer

Hannes and Jane Gebauer

Needless to say, I have no doubt the Catholic Church is the one true Church. The Catholic Church existed well before any of the other churches in the world today. That in itself is grounds for my Catholic conviction - the other churches can't claim to be the one true Church because they didn't exist. But I believe the road to salvation can be entered at a number of different churches.

Many years ago there was a Catholic doctrine that there was no salvation outside the Church. People don't talk like that any more, or at least I hope they don't, because we should respect people of different faiths.

If an Anglican has no call to the Catholic Church, he or she should stay put. But if conversion to Catholicism niggles at him or her, than something should be done about it - there should be a positive answer to the call. The same should be said about the followers of a number of other churches. If they have faith and are in a state of grace, they have the same opportunity to get eternal life as Catholics.

A story to break the ice when introduced to Christians from different churches is that of Saint Peter showing a Protestant around Heaven. The pair come across a big fortress. "Shush, you best be quiet," Saint Peter said. "The Catholics are inside there and they think they're the only ones up here."

I also think people who have no religion or who have stopped going to church can get eternal life.

God alone judges.

As sad as I find it when someone gives up going to church, I realise that person may be facing obstacles which seem impossible to overcome.

No one is without sin.

Everybody makes mistakes during life's journey.

If we make a blue, we should try to learn from it and move on - not get bogged down in the problems of the past but look towards the future and be determined to improve.

The Lord warned us against judging one another. He said

that with the same judgment you judge people you will be judged yourself. In other words, if you are harsh in judging other people you can expect to receive harsh judgment. We must encourage each other to be positive and to grow in God's light.

The Western world, in particular, is getting more technologically advanced every day. Much is made of the good aspects of this development, but it also brings problems and leads to sin. The more technology we have the less jobs there seems to be. The less jobs the more crime, though this is a simplification because it could be argued that the job and crime rates are not directly related.

As with all things in life, governments need to include God in decisions. A major challenge looming for federal governments in Western countries is that of cloning. How far should scientists be allowed to go? My personal view is that God will intervene before humans are cloned. Perhaps this intervention will come from the mouths of our political leaders as God works through them.

It is a good move to call on God for guidance, but we should also remember to give Him thanks and include Him in happy times. God should be a part of every aspect of our life.

Priests have set prayer times during the day so they probably find it easier than the average layman to focus on God. I think most people would find it useful to put aside 10-15 minutes in the morning and at night for prayer. That sort of discipline would ensure that God is not sidelined because of work, family and other distractions.

Bible studies are held regularly in a lot of parishes to give people the chance to learn more about God and to join in a prayer group. These meetings are a good way to focus on the Lord, but they're only effective if the group leader is an experienced guide.

The Bible has been interpreted in different ways, some of which have been misleading, so it is vital that study groups are

Pope John Paul chats with Benedictine monk Father Stephen and Father Lisle

steered towards the right paths. It has been my experience that people who try to interpret the Bible without help can end up off the track.

I have spent many quiet times before God at the monastery in New Norcia. It is one of my favourite places, if not my favourite, when I go on retreat. The Benedictine monks live a simple life under the guidance of Abbot Placid Spearritt - they're largely self-sufficient and there is no radio or television to distract them. I like to pray with them at their regular prayer times as well as spend some time alone before God to think about what He has done for me and what He wants me to do for Him. The monastery's peace and tranquillity helps me to reflect on life and to ask God for help to make up a list of priorities.

For a number years, the monks have opened the monastery's doors to the laity at weekends and at other times. Many people who have spent a few days with the monks say they are spiritually richer for the experience.

One of the most memorable and enriching experiences I have had, meeting the Pope when he visited Perth in 1986, was shared with the monks.

The Way, Truth and Life

God has a plan for every one of us and we should put our trust in Him. I recommend taking five minutes from the world's distractions to think about what God could be calling you to do.

There is only one way that I have got true direction in life - by putting my trust in Jesus. When I wake in the morning, I thank Jesus for bringing me to the start of a new day. In the same way at night Jesus is never far from my mind and prayer never far from my lips. My relationship with Jesus has sustained me and enabled me to grow spiritually during my life.

Jesus is the star of the achievements in my life and every day I live to serve the Lord is another bonus from Him.

At 83, the curtain is closing on the story of my life.

And so Father I thank You through Jesus Christ Your Son for a wonderful journey of many years. I thank You for the opportunity to serve many different people in the Bahamas, South Africa, England and Australia. I thank You, above all, for the gift of faith which brought me to the Church founded by our Lord Jesus Christ. All glory and honour to You Father, Son and Holy Spirit, and to the Immaculate Mother of God. Amen.

Bibliography

Allitt, Patrick. Catholic Converts: British and American Intellectuals Turn to Rome, lthaca and London: Cornell University Press, 1997.

Augustine. Confessions. Translated with an Introduction and Notes by Henry Chadwick. Oxford [etc.]: Oxford University Press, 1991.

Follow the Footnote or The Advocate as Historian of Same-Sex Marriage, P. Lubin and D. Duncan. 47 Catholic *University Law Review* 1271 (1998).

Hollis, Crispian. Catholic Oxford. London: Catholic Truth Society, 1974

Jaki, Stanley L. The One True Fold: Newman and His Converts. Royal Oak, Michigan: Real View Books, 1998.

Ker, Ian ed. Newman and Conversion. Edinburgh: T and T Clark, 1997.

Madrid, Patrick, ed. Surprised by Truth: Eleven Converts Give the Biblical and Historical Reasons for Becoming Catholic. San Diego: Basilica Press, 1994.

Year in Review 1993: Religion, Encyclopaedia Britannica Online.

Dogmatic Constitution on the Church (Lumen Gentium) 1964 CTS Do349.

Decree on Ecumenism (Unitatis Redintegratio) 1965 CTS Do351

Directory for the Application of Principals and Norms on Ecumenism, 1993 CTS Do615.

Ut Unum Sint, 1995 CTS Do636.

One Bread One Body, Catholic Bishops' Conferences (England & Wales, Scotland, Ireland) 1998.

Presiding Bishop's Letter on the Lambeth Conference's Sexuality Resolution (Frank T. Griswold), 1998.

Resolution 1.10, Lambeth Conference, 1998.

Resolution 8, Lambeth Conference, 1988.

Mokgethi Motlhabi, 1986. The Theory and Practice of Black Resistance to Apartheid - a social ethical analysis. Johannesburg: Skotaville Publishers.

Rob Davies, Dan O'Meara and Sipho Dlamini, 1985. The Struggle for South Africa - a reference guide to movements, organisations and institutions, Volume 2. London: Zed Books.

Allan Boesak, 1984. Black and Reformed - Apartheid, Liberation and the Calvanist Tradition. Johannesburg: Skotaville Publishers.

Allan Boesak, 1977. Farewell to Innocence. Kampen: JH Kok

Johann Kinghorn (ed), 1986. Die NG Kerk en Apartheid (The Dutch Reformed Church in South Africa and Apartheid) Johannesburg: Macmillan.

John de Gruchy and Charles Villa-Vicencio, 1983, Apartheid is a Heresy. Cape Town: David Philip Publisher.

Itumeleng J Mosala and Buti Tlhagale, 1986. The Unquestionable Right to be Free. Johannesburg: Skotaville Publishers.

AN Pelzer, 1963. Verwoerd aan Die Word (Verwoerd Speaks). Pretoria: APB.

Nederduitse Gereformeerde Kerk. Algemene Sinode. 1974. Ras Volk en Nasie en Volkereverhoudinge in die lig van die Skrif. Kaapstad NGKU.

Nederduitse Gereformeerde Kerk. Algemene Sinode. 1986. Kerk en Samelewing. 'n Getuienis van die Ned. Geref. Kerk. Bloemfontein: Algemene Sinodale Kommissie.

Nederduitse Gereformeerde Kerk. Algemene Sinode. 1990. Kerk en Samelewing. 'n Getuienis van die Ned. Geref. Kerk. Bloemfontein: Algemene Sinodale Kommissie.